the abiding way

Books by Jeanine Amapola Ward

Becoming Happy & Healthy

the abiding way

A 40-DAY DEVOTIONAL STUDY THROUGH THE GOSPEL OF JOHN

JEANINE AMAPOLA WARD

BETHANYHOUSE
a division of Baker Publishing Group
Minneapolis, Minnesota

Published by Bethany House Publishers
Minneapolis, Minnesota
BethanyHouse.com

Bethany House Publishers is a division of
Baker Publishing Group, Grand Rapids, Michigan

Printed in the United States of America

Cover design by Lindy Kasler

Published in association with The Bindery Agency, TheBinderyAgency.com.

Baker Publishing Group publications use paper produced from sustainable forestry practices and postconsumer waste whenever possible.

26 27 28 29 30 31 32 7 6 5 4 3 2 1

To my husband, Kaleb, and my son, Duke.
I love you both so much.
Abide in Him in all you do,
and you will be blessed.

Contents

Introduction

Let's be honest—being a woman today can feel *exhausting*. Buy this, do that, look this way, talk like this, don't say that, try harder, do more, don't be like *her* . . . It's overwhelming. It feels like running a race with no finish line. The world keeps shouting for you to do more while your soul is quietly begging for rest.

But what if the solution isn't found in *doing more* . . . but actually in doing *less* and just simply being with Jesus?

If you're feeling burned out, spiritually dry, or unsure how to actually connect with Jesus in your real, everyday life, this devotional is for you. These forty days are designed to meet you right where you are, not where you think you should be. Whether you are new to the faith or you've known Jesus for years, you'll find space here to breathe, rest, and connect with God—the One who brings true peace. My prayer is that by the end of this journey, you'll no longer feel like you're performing for God, but instead walking intimately with Him. You'll know more of the heart and character of Jesus, because ultimately, this is all about Him.

By the time you complete this devotional, we will have gone through the entire Gospel of John together. We have so much to learn. The book of John is amazing!

But this isn't just about learning more—it's about *living more connected* to the Vine.

It's about abiding.

That's the heart behind *The Abiding Way*. This devotional is not just another thing to check off your to-do list, but something to help lift the weight. A breath of fresh air. A return to the source of life itself. What you're holding isn't just paper and ink—it's something I've prayed over for years and have lived out myself. And now it's in your hands.

This book was born from my own crazy and beautiful journey with Jesus. In 2019, when I truly surrendered my life to Him, a good friend—someone prophetic and deeply Spirit-led—gave me a necklace with the word *Abide* on it. I didn't even know what that meant at the time! I ran home and Googled it, and the definition I found felt . . . underwhelming. "To accept or act in accordance with a rule." That didn't feel very inspiring. But my friend intended to communicate a truth that went much deeper. She was pointing me to the biblical meaning of *abide*—a word that would shape the rest of my walk with Jesus. And it's a word I want to pass on to you.

Abide comes from John 15 and means to remain, to dwell, to linger, to stay connected. And trust me, it's not just a convenient word—it's a lifeline. It changed my life. So much so, I built a ministry around it. I started Abide Tribe in 2020 to help other women experience the freedom and joy of walking closely with Jesus, providing weekly Bible studies and merch to wear as a reminder, and now . . . this devotional.

Even more than that single word—*abide*—the entire Gospel of John changed my life. It was the first book of the Bible I ever fully read, and the one that helped me fall in love with Jesus. John's Gospel is rich, unique, and full of stories you won't find in the other Gospels. The truth is, we can't walk closely with Jesus unless we learn to abide in Him. And in a world that's loud and hurried, abiding can feel like swimming upstream. But it's worth it. And it's what this forty-day journey is all about.

Each day, you'll dive into Scripture from the book of John, unpack a key theme from the passage, learn a new trait about Jesus, and reflect on how it applies to your life. This isn't a means to simply accumulate head knowledge—it's deep heart transformation. Each day you'll receive teaching, truth, and space to reflect through journal prompts, and you'll also have space to pause, reflect, and pray. My hope is that your guided time in the Word feels personal, doable, and deeply refreshing. I pray that you leave knowing Jesus more and knowing how to abide in Him even deeper.

Before you begin each devotional, I encourage you to take a moment and pray something like this: "Lord, I give you this time. Open my heart and my eyes. Reveal more of yourself to me, and help me apply your truth to my life. Amen."

By the end of these forty days, my prayer is that you'll be less focused on striving and more rooted in abiding. That you'll feel lighter, more at peace, more in love with Jesus, and more confident in His Word. That is, indeed, *The Abiding Way*.

So, get comfy. Grab a cozy drink. Put your phone on Do Not Disturb. This is sacred space. You're not just reading a book—you're stepping into an invitation to know Jesus deeper and rest in Him like never before.

Let's go!

Day 1

Jesus, the Living Word of God

Reading: John 1:1–26

Key Verse: "In the beginning was the Word, and the Word was with God, and the Word was God. He was in the beginning with God. All things were made through him, and without him was not any thing made that was made. In him was life, and the life was the light of men. The light shines in the darkness, and the darkness has not overcome it."—John 1:1–5

As we begin this devotional, let's start with the questions *Who even is Jesus? Why does He matter so much?* If we don't understand this fundamental truth, the rest of the book won't mean much. Let's start with *Who is Jesus to you?* Think about some adjectives to describe Him. There's no right or wrong answer—it's based on your experience.

For me, Jesus is Savior, friend, safety, my comfort, my helper, my hope, and my joy! It's okay if you didn't know what to write or if your list was short. By the end of this devotional, I believe you'll have a long list.

If you are a Christ-follower, you know Jesus to be the Son of God and Savior of the world, but in this opening Scripture, we read that Jesus is *the Word*. How is this possible? How can something intangible be something tangible? The word John uses here is the Greek word *logos*, which means "a word uttered by a living voice."* This living Word (Jesus) was in the beginning (eternal), was with God (in close relationship), and was God (equal with Him). Does this remind you of the creation story in Genesis 1:1? John is using similar language to tell us that in the beginning, along with God, Jesus existed before He descended to earth. Jesus came into the world incarnate (in human form), yet He was still fully God. This is a wild concept to grasp!

Many of us think that Jesus being born through Mary was His first time entering this world, yet the Bible says He was here in the beginning with God and that He was a part of creating creation (Colossians 1:16)! Many of us attribute creation only to God the Father, but Jesus was also there because He is a part of the Trinity (Father, Son, and Holy Spirit). Jesus being defined as the Word explains His divinity, meaning He is fully God and possesses the nature, attributes, and authority of God. It signifies that Jesus is not merely a human prophet, teacher, or moral leader, but God Himself.

John 1:14 states, "The Word became flesh and made his dwelling among us" (NIV). He became like *us* for *us*. He came to earth to identify with us, be with us, and know us. No other god does this. No other gods come to dwell with people, humble themselves, serve them, and require nothing from them but to repent, believe, and be saved from their sins. This is a huge distinction between the Christian faith and other religions. Jesus became like us and came to serve, not be served.

This hopefully awakens your heart and gives you appreciation for the fact that God gave us His very Word (in Christ) to help us know Him more and have tools to fight back against the enemy in this difficult life. It makes me thankful that I have something to hold onto when life throws storms my way. During the most difficult seasons of my life, I quite literally held onto my Bible as a safety blanket when I felt scared or alone, and I encourage you to do the same, despite how weird it may feel.

John also states in this chapter that Jesus is our Life and Light (v. 4)—two recurring words you'll see throughout this book. Jesus came to give us life abundantly, a life that is more than just existing. He brings our dead souls and dead situations back to life. He is where we find light, even in the darkest hours, even when there seems to be no hope. He wants to be your life and light, no matter what you are going through. All you need to do is believe in Him and call upon Him to become His child (v. 12).

Pause and Reflect

Child of God is our identity above anything else—above our job title, relationship status, sorority, gender, degree, or any other label that we (or others) place on ourselves. Is there an area of your life that sometimes becomes your primary identity, taking the rightful place of God? Reflect on what might be stealing your time and attention away from the Lord.

The one true living God wants to dwell with you through Christ. *Dwell* is a synonym for *abide*. He wants to live in you, be with you, and remain in you. Are you a good home for Him to dwell in? Is He welcome in *all* areas of your life, not just the ones you want to invite Him into? Is He allowed to speak to you and mold you to look more like Him? It's easy to give Him access to the areas that seem safe, but can you surrender and give Him the ones that aren't? That's what abiding is—giving Him all of you and trusting Him with your whole being. He's a good Father who knows how to handle and take care of you. Trust Him to do so.

I pray you now know just a little more of who Jesus is—the true life and light our souls long for. Nothing else will do.

Prayer

Father, thank You for giving us something on earth to tangibly hold onto even when everything else feels fleeting. I thank You that You came to dwell among us as the Word made flesh so that I may never feel alone. Refine me so that I may fully believe this and fully welcome You into my heart to be a place You can dwell. Show me areas of my life that need surrender. I pray that I will receive the full joy of Your promise and pass it on to others. Thank You for who You are. Amen.

Reflection Questions

1. How does Jesus being the Word change the way you read your Bible from here on out?

2. What did you learn about Jesus in the first chapter of John?

Day 2

Jesus, the One Who Sees and Knows You

Reading: John 1:29–51

Key Verse: "How do you know me?" Nathanael asked. Jesus answered, "I saw you while you were still under the fig tree before Philip called you."—John 1:48 NIV

Have you ever walked into a room full of people you don't know and felt unbearably awkward? You hide in the corner and start scanning the room, hoping you might recognize *one* person. What's even more awkward is when someone comes up to you and says, "Hi! It's SO good to see you!" And your mind goes absolutely blank—*How do I know this person?*—as you frantically try to remember their name. (I hate to admit this, but I am horrible at remembering people's names. It's something I'm working on, okay?) Now, imagine someone comes up to you, someone who knows a thousand things about you, yet you don't even know their name. It might be a bit shocking, right? Well, that's how Jesus is. He knows everything about us—intricately, intimately, and intentionally—even if we don't know Him at all.

In today's reading, Jesus meets a man named Nathanael, also called Bartholomew. He is one of Jesus' first disciples. Jesus displays His supernatural power of knowledge to Nathanael by telling him He knows him, where he's from, qualities about him, and what he was doing, even when Nathanael didn't know Jesus was watching. Nathanael responds in shock, saying, "How do you know me?" Jesus says, "I saw you." This confirmed to Nathanael that Jesus truly was the Messiah (the Anointed and Chosen One) they had been waiting for. How else could someone know this information? It's not like anyone had hidden cameras or all of Nathanael's information hanging out in his Instagram bio.

Pause and Reflect

Do you ever feel hidden from God? Does it ever feel like God isn't picking up the telephone? *Hello? Anyone there?* *Silence* If that sounds familiar, share when you felt that way:

I love this section of John because it reminds us that God hears and sees us even when we don't hear or see Him. This may sometimes feel like a one-sided relationship in which we are doing all the effort, but God has known and seen you *before* you were born. Jeremiah 1:5 says, "Before I formed you in the womb I knew you, before you were born I set you apart; I appointed you as a prophet to the nations" (NIV). This verse may be written about Jeremiah, but it applies to you too. God not only formed and knew you, but chose you and set you apart, before you were even born! He knows you intricately, intimately, and intentionally. You were created on purpose. You are not an accident. This truth makes me emotional, because I often stand in front of the mirror and pick myself apart, criticizing my flaws. But God gently reminds me, "I formed you."

The Creator of the universe knows you by name. He knows every hair on your head, every thought, all your flaws, all your talents, all the insecurities you may feel. And He *still* chooses you. This may cause one of two reactions:

1. Fear—Someone is watching me 24/7 and I don't want them to see who I *truly* am.
2. Comfort—God sees me, even when I feel unworthy of love or being chosen. He loves me with an everlasting love, despite my flaws and sins. He loves me enough to stick around forever.

I hope you picked number two, because that's the truth. God loves you, even when He sees your sin and "ugly" sides.

Sometimes God will give what I call little "God-winks" to let you know He sees you. When you experience those God-winks, think of Him asking you a question, like Jesus asked Nathanael: "Do you believe me?"

Friend, do you believe? Do you believe He sees you?

An example of a God-wink in my life happened when I took my son to the doctor. My car was in the shop, so I Ubered to the appointment. Once my appointment ended, the front-desk ladies refused to let me Uber home with my baby, so one of them offered to drive me home. On the ride home, she told me she was an event planner—someone I specifically had been looking for because I wanted to host local events for women, but it was overwhelming to do it alone. It felt like an answered prayer, because after that ride, she and I planned a Bible study event in Oklahoma for women—something that had been on my heart.

God reminded me that He cares. God was letting me know, "I see your desires and care about the little things you don't think I see." He cares for you too. He is preparing people and places for you in advance. Now, I know an event planner is not a life-changing need. Some of you are praying for far bigger miracles. I've been there too. But this moment was God's reminder that if He sees the tiny, ordinary desires of my heart, then I can trust that He also sees the heavy, impossible ones too.

Think of a time when God showed you that He saw you. It can be a big or small thing.

Anytime you begin to doubt or ask, "Does God really care or see me?" think of this story of Nathanael. The more you press into Him, the more He will reveal Himself to you. James 4:8 says, "Draw near to God, and he will draw near to you." Matthew 7:7–8 says, "Ask and it will be given to you; seek and you will find; knock and the door will be opened to you. For everyone who asks receives; the one who seeks finds; and to the one who knocks, the door will be opened" (NIV). God is not far when we seek Him with our whole hearts. Sometimes He doesn't answer right away or in the way you expect. But can you still choose to seek and pursue Him even when He doesn't answer in the manner or time you prefer? Following God is not a linear path; it's a long path with daily steps of faithfulness.

Let this be your reminder that God sees every tear, worry, anxiety, fear, doubt, and question. On top of that, He can handle it. All He is asking you is, "Do you believe me? Do you trust me?" I pray you can believe that God is the God who sees—not just Nathanael, but you too.

Prayer

Father, thank You for seeing me. You have never left me or forsaken me. I praise You that I am not alone, that You walk through the darkest of valleys with me. That even when I don't feel You close to me, You are near. You love me intricately, intimately, and intentionally. I pray that I trust You through all my questions and fears. As I come to You with those questions, I pray that I am attentive to Your answer. Draw near to me as I draw near to You. Amen.

Reflection Questions

1. What is an area of your life where you need Jesus to see you?

2. What fears, doubts, or worries are you still holding onto that you need to give to God?

Day 3

Jesus, the Perfect Provider

Reading: John 2:1–25

Key Verse: "When the wine ran out, the mother of Jesus said to him, 'They have no wine.'"—John 2:3

Being told no really stinks sometimes. Being told you can't have something that you've strongly desired for a long time hurts even more. Maybe that thing you want is a spouse, a home, a baby, a job you've been waiting for, a positive health test result, or an acceptance letter. Who likes to hear no? Certainly not me.

In this chapter of John, there was a wedding in Cana, and the hosts run out of wine. Jesus and his friends were guests at the wedding. Jesus' mother tells her son about the wine shortage, and He responds by saying to her, "My hour has not yet come." What He meant by this is that it was not the right time for Him to start His ministry, which would ultimately lead to His crucifixion—His main purpose for being on earth. Jesus was not ready to reveal that He was the coming Messiah they had all been waiting for.

Yet Jesus sees this need for more wine and then fills it, though He chooses to do so privately. He turns water to wine at this feast so the celebrations can continue. Water signifies the Old Covenant purification.

Wine signifies Christ's sacrificial blood. This moment foreshadowed the blood that would be drawn from Jesus during His death on the cross (Luke 22:20). His perfect sacrifice would have the power to cleanse men and women of their sins once and for all, from the inside out. This moment is no small thing.

Here's another reason why: Jesus cares about our needs and desires. When He sees a lack, He fills it with abundance. It's part of His very nature. This water-to-wine miracle at the wedding is Jesus' first recorded miracle. Additionally, it's the first of seven signs that John describes to prove that Jesus is the Messiah.

The water-to-wine miracle revealed how Jesus can draw something extraordinary out of the ordinary. Picture the servants. Moments earlier, those jars held nothing but water, and now they overflowed with the finest wine. They surely would have been in awe. The proof was undeniable. Lack became abundance. What was empty was filled.

Pause here for a moment and ask yourself: "What is lacking in my life that I need Jesus to fill?" Maybe it's joy, peace, hope for a circumstance you've given up on, finances, friends who support you, or reconciliation with a parent. Take a few moments to write about your circumstances and invite God into them.

What I know about Jesus' character is that nothing He does is an accident, and He sees places of lack and restores them—places where someone else might give up, but you feel in your spirit that you need to keep going. Your circumstances may change for the worst, but Jesus hasn't. God is the same God who sees brokenness, identifies the places where you might be running out, and then generously fills those places for you. Now the example in this chapter—wine—might seem like less of a need and more of a want, but it shows that Jesus cares about our little desires, even the seemingly inconsequential ones you bring to Him. You are not a burden to Him. You're not asking too much of Him. He wants you, as His child, to come to Him and know He that will supply *every* need you have, even the small ones. Philippians 4:19 says, "And my God will supply all your needs according to His riches in glory in Christ Jesus."

Not only does God give to His people, but He gives exceedingly and abundantly more than they could ask for when they seek Him (Ephesians 3:20). This is your encouragement to reopen the prayer journal that maybe you've shut for a long time and restart those prayers, praying earnestly until something happens. Seeking Him with your whole heart, soul, mind, and strength is not always simple, but it is the path of intimacy with God. We press in. We pray. We seek Him even in the storm. And sometimes He does not answer in the way we hoped—or in the timing we pray for. But God's decisions are never without purpose. God's delays or denials are often the result of His protection or redirection, even when we can't see it yet.

What matters most is who we become while we wait. Sometimes God says no because He's still transforming us, strengthening us, or preparing us for what's ahead. The question becomes, Do we trust that He's in the driver's seat, or do we insist on taking the wheel? Letting Him be the driver requires us to let go, surrender, have faith, and trust Him.

Pause and Reflect

What does God need to change in you first before He changes the situation?

The more you surrender, the more freedom you'll feel. The miracle worker hasn't changed. God still turns water to wine in our wildest moments, but maybe the change needs to start with *you*. Maybe He wants to work on you first before He works on your situation. Trust Him to touch and shape all the hardened areas of your life, because when He does, you come out better and look more like Him, which is the goal of being a Christ-follower! Invite Him in to do so.

Just as this miracle strengthened the disciples' faith (John 2:11), your story may produce the same result for someone watching your life. What might God do if you kept pressing in and praying? The outcome may not look exactly like you imagined, but God always works for His glory and for the good of those who love Him. He's still in business of transforming ordinary moments, broken places, and empty jars into something beautiful.

Keep seeking Him. Keep asking. How will you know until you try? Your faithfulness might become the very testimony that leads someone else to believe that God is still a miracle worker.

Prayer

Jesus, thank You that Your miracles have not ceased. Lord, I need a miracle. I need hope. Help me trust You along this process. I pray, Father, that I would look to You for all my needs and bring all my needs to the cross. Help change me along this way to look more like You. Help me trust that when You say no, it's for my good. Thank You that You are still working, even when I don't see it. I love you. Amen.

Reflection Questions

1. What situation do you need Jesus to revive for you?

2. What has caused you to doubt God's provision, and what did you hear today that could help change that?

Day 4

Jesus, the Giver of New Life

Reading: John 3:1–15

Key Verse: "Jesus answered him, 'Truly, truly, I say to you, unless one is born again he cannot see the kingdom of God.'"—John 3:3 NIV

Growing up in a Christian home, I *thought* I was following Jesus, but my actions didn't reflect it. One day, someone who wasn't a Christian called me out: "Aren't you a Christian? If so, why are you drinking and partying?" That question left me feeling deeply guilty, yet challenged. Was I really living the life I claimed? The answer unfortunately was no. It wasn't until I understood what it meant to be born again that my life changed. I thought I had freedom by doing whatever I wanted whenever I wanted, but in reality, my soul was decaying. I spent my life performing—trying to appear righteous to my parents, peers, and people online—but secretly I was living in darkness. When I finally decided to give my life to Christ in 2019 and surrendered my heart to Him, everything changed. *I needed a heart transformation, not just behavior modification.*

In John 3, Nicodemus asks Jesus, "How can a man be born again?" No one had heard this concept before. He wondered, "Can he enter a second time into his mother's womb and be born?" (v. 3). But Jesus wasn't speaking of physical rebirth; He was talking about spiritual rebirth. For years, the Israelites followed strict laws, sacrifices, and rituals to atone for their sins. Blood was always required in atonement, so they sacrificed animals, specifically lambs, and these lambs had to be spotless and without flaw. The Israelites' faith was focused on behavior, obedience, and sacrifices. But Jesus came to fulfill the law—not abolish it—offering the perfect solution for salvation. Through His sacrifice on the cross, He granted us the ability for true spiritual rebirth, no longer requiring us to sacrifice for our own sins. Jesus became the final sacrifice, hence why He's called the Lamb of God.

Many people claim to be saved, or believe they are, but don't fully grasp what it means to be born again. Maybe, like me, you grew up Christian or have been half-in with God. But being born again is a personal choice. At some point, each of us must choose to accept Christ of our own free will. You didn't choose to be born physically, but you must choose to be reborn spiritually.

Choosing Christ means fully surrendering your heart to Him and turning away from sin. Second Corinthians 5:17 states, "Therefore, if anyone is in Christ, he is a new creation. The old has passed away; behold, the new has come." When you accept Christ, your old self is gone—you are born again! Your past sins are wiped clean, and your life is made new in Him. This new birth isn't something we achieve through human effort—it is by God's grace through faith (Titus 3:5). Rebirth is an internal transformation when God captures your heart, leading you to repentance and dependence on Him.

If we don't fully understand this, we might fall into the trap of performing for God—trying to earn our salvation rather than trusting in Jesus' finished work. You might rely on your parents' salvation, your friends, or your good deeds to feel saved, but salvation isn't a feeling. Jesus said, "That which is born of the flesh is flesh, and that which is born of the Spirit is spirit" (John 3:6). It's your spirit being miraculously renewed by the Holy Spirit. Often, we try to work our way to salvation, thinking that if we just read our Bibles more, serve more, pray more . . . But Jesus isn't after our good deeds—He's after our hearts. When we truly encounter Jesus, our actions will follow naturally because our hearts have been changed.

Pause and Reflect

Maybe you're reading this and wondering, *Am I truly saved?* Ask yourself this: "If my life ended today, where would my soul go . . . and why do I believe that?" Write your honest thoughts below.

If your answer is based on your actions rather than what Jesus did, you may be missing the heart of the Gospel. There's no shame in this—only an opportunity for clarity. Jesus is the only one who can give new life (Romans 10:9). Salvation isn't about what *we* do, but about what *He* did. You don't need to be perfect to come to Jesus. He welcomes you as you are and cleans you up as you stay. He's just waiting for you to surrender your heart. This should bring a deep sigh of relief, because if our salvation was up to us being perfect, none of us would be saved! We are saved by grace, through faith (Ephesians 2:8–9).

When I went all in with Jesus, my heart changed. I experienced freedom and peace like never before. That is my desire for you too. Maybe you feel like you've tried but still aren't sure of your future. I pray this message brings you peace and truth. Jesus told Nicodemus in John 3:15 "that whoever believes in Him [will] have eternal life." Jesus gives you one

Way to heaven out of His kindness—not out of exclusivity—so you don't have to wander aimlessly looking for the true Way (John 14:6). He is the Way you are looking for, and this Way is for *all* who call upon His name.

If you've never accepted Christ as your Lord and Savior, today can be your day. This is a chance for you to either rededicate your life to Him or go all in and choose to surrender your life to Him. If you're ready to choose Jesus and make the best decision of your life, say this prayer with me.

"Dear Heavenly Father, I come to You as a sinner. I ask for Your forgiveness, and I believe that Your Son, Jesus, died for my sins and rose again. I now turn away from sin and invite Jesus into my heart to be my Lord and Savior. I give my life to Him. Amen."

If you gave your life to Jesus, welcome to the kingdom! Angels are rejoicing. Take a moment to remember this special day.

Date and sign below the following:

Today I accepted Christ and surrendered my life to Him.

Prayer

Father God, I pray for a deeper revelation of the new life You offer. You aren't asking me to perform for You—You want my heart. So here it is. Take all of it. Remove any unbelief or fear in me. Help me to honor and seek You with my whole heart. Thank You, Jesus, for giving me new life. I trust you. Amen.

Reflection Questions

1. What areas of your life are you not yet *all* in with God?

2. Do you believe you are saved? If so, why? If not, why not? If you still aren't sure, meet with a trusted spiritual mentor, friend, or pastor so you can be assured of your salvation.

Day 5

Jesus, the One Who Comes to Save, Not Condemn

Reading: John 3:15–36

Key Verse: "For God did not send his Son into the world to condemn the world, but to save the world through him."—John 3:17 NIV

When I was three years old, I almost drowned. I was at my friend's house, and she decided that today was the day she'd take my sisters and me on a swim. The problem? None of us even knew how to swim. And yet, with full confidence, she said, "Let's go!" and we all jumped into the pool, hand-in-hand. I remember, even as a three-year-old, this impending feeling of doom as I flailed around in the water, kicking my legs and trying to find my way up somehow.

Moments later, I saw my friend's mom in her purple workout outfit jump into the pool and pull us out one by one. She saved us all! Gasping for air, I regained my breath. *Phew.* Thankfully, we weren't in there long enough for something drastic to happen, but praise God that my friend's mom was close by the window that afternoon, or I'm not sure if my sisters or I would be here today. Trust me, we all got swim lessons shortly after that!

What stands out to me now, as I remember this story, is that the mom didn't scold us. She didn't yell, "What were you thinking?" Instead, she frantically asked us, "Are you all okay?!" Her first response was concern. Compassion. Rescue. That moment stuck with me—not only just because it was terrifying, but because it mirrored something far deeper. My soul has felt like that before—drowning in shame, overwhelmed by sin, desperate for rescue. And just like that day, someone stepped in. Someone saved me. That someone was Jesus.

Pause and Reflect

Do you feel like you are drowning today? Are you overwhelmed? In what area of your life do you need rescue?

John 3:16 might be the most popular and well-known Bible verse ever, but if you don't fully understand the gravity of it, it will only be words on a page. This verse is pivotal to our lives because this is the essence of the gospel. God deeply loved us, saw we were drowning in sin, and wanted to be our rescuer. But before we rush past these familiar words, it helps to sit with the imagery Jesus is inviting us to see: God noticing us struggling, unable to save ourselves, and choosing to enter the water with us. Salvation wasn't an abstract concept to Him. It was personal, intentional, and driven by love.

But it's John 3:17 that hits me the hardest. People tend to believe this misconception that God is a judgmental, finger-pointing, shaming God. That all He wants to do is make you feel guilty, tell you to go to church, and point out all your flaws. But the Bible quite literally tells us that

He doesn't come to *condemn* us, but to *save* us. He moves toward us with rescue, not rebuke. He doesn't lecture us while we're barely keeping our heads above water, but pulls us close and brings us safely back to shore.

Maybe you need to hear that right now. Jesus doesn't condemn you. He isn't mad at you. But He also doesn't want you to stay in your sin, because he knows sin kills, robs, and slowly pulls you under. Maybe you've been running from Him or have been carrying shame for far too long. Maybe you feel like you're drowning in guilt and shame over past or current decisions. Maybe you're drowning in pain from incredibly difficult circumstances you've been dealing with and feel like no one seems to truly care. Jesus is the rescue you've been looking for.

I was living in the very darkness John 3:19 speaks of—and Jesus saved me. He didn't show up with a list of my mistakes. He came with outstretched arms and a rescue plan. If there's one thing I know about Jesus, it's that He isn't exclusive. If He could rescue me, He can rescue you too. Many of us are walking in darkness—some knowingly, some unknowingly. But God wants to pull you out of the waters you're drowning in, greeting you not with condemnation, but with compassion. That's who He is.

Romans 2:4 reminds us that it's God's kindness that leads us to repentance. His kindness doesn't excuse sin, but it meets us in it and pulls us out. You don't have to fix yourself first. You don't have to be your own savior. Jesus already has that title—and He's really good at it. All you have to do is ask and accept the help. Whatever you're drowning in—shame, guilt, fear, anxiety—He's ready to rescue you. Tell Him how much you need Him now.

Prayer

Jesus, show me the places in my life where I still need saving. Reveal where I've been trying to be my own hero. I invite You into my situation—help me stop striving and start surrendering. Give me the courage to be honest with You, with myself, and with others about where I'm weak and in need of healing. Rescue me, Lord. I know You can. In Your powerful name, amen.

Reflection Questions

1. Are there any parts of your life where you're still trying to be your own savior? Why is it hard for you to surrender those areas to Jesus?

2. Think back to a time when you felt rescued. How does that moment mirror the way Jesus rescues your soul?

Day 6

Jesus, the Living Water

Reading: John 4:1-18

Key Verse: "Everyone who drinks this water will soon become thirsty again, but whoever drinks the water I give them will never thirst. Indeed, the water I give them will become in them a spring of water welling up to eternal life."—John 4:14 NIV

John 4 is one of my favorite chapters in the Gospel of John because it shows us how deeply Jesus cares about our well-being, and how He will go out of his way to meet us. Jesus encounters a woman at a well who has a secret past and current sin. He didn't need to take this path to meet with this woman, since Jews typically avoided this region, but He knew there was someone there who needed His healing. Jesus lovingly and truthfully calls this woman out on her sin to set her free. He longed for her to find the freedom only He offers.

Many of us are like this woman—buried in sin, hiding in isolation to avoid judgment, and running back to the same old things, hoping to find relief or comfort in all the wrong places. I remember when I was like her too, clinging to toxic relationships and going to the bars for an escape from my pain, but my vices left me feeling worse than they found me. Money, relationships, success, and fleeting pleasures may be the wells we rely on, but they can never fill the God-sized hole in our souls. They will only leave us empty and desperate for more.

Pause and Reflect

If Jesus came looking for you today, where would he find you? What "wells" are you relying on today that aren't satisfying you at a soul-deep level?

In Jesus' day, a Jewish man would normally avoid Samaritans altogether —centuries of ethnic, religious, and social hostility kept them apart. A rabbi especially would never interact publicly with a woman, and certainly not a Samaritan woman with a known broken past. Yet Jesus intentionally walked through Samaria, sat beside her in the middle of the day, and asked her for a drink. He speaks to her first. His initiation of the conversation shows that He doesn't wait for us to be "clean," sin-free, or qualified in some way to be in His presence. It also makes my heart so tender knowing that Jesus was treating this woman with dignity, by approaching her first. In the culture at the time, women often went unheard, and yet Jesus gave her a voice and invited her into conversation. In fact, as you go deeper, you'll see that He wasn't just inviting her into any random conversation; He was essentially inviting her into a *theological* conversation—something usually reserved for rabbis and "worthy" males.

Let's see how this unfolds.

After being asked a question by Jesus, the woman answered the question with a question. (Haven't we all done that in our conversations, or is that just me?) She asks him in verse 9, "How can you ask me for a drink?" The reason she asked? Because she knew that Jews and Samaritans didn't associate with one another. Jesus then answered her question, "If you knew the gift of God and who it is that asks you for a drink, you would have asked him and he would have given you living water" (John 4:10 NIV). And this woman responded, "Give me that water." She assumed it was something tangible to satisfy her need. But Jesus offered her something far greater—Himself. He is the Living Water that brings true healing and freedom. It's alive, not limited to a place or moment, and it's offered to you too. She even leaves her bucket of water at the well, signifying that she got what she needed, and then she runs and tells others about her encounter, leading others to Jesus too!

This is what Jesus does—He initiates with you. He takes your empty, broken wells and fills them with His satisfying water. He knows your past, pain, and problems, and goes out of His way to heal them. Whatever you might be dealing with—sin, heartbreak, grief, loneliness—depend on Him instead of returning to broken wells that will never satisfy. If you let Him be the sustaining water you are looking for, you will flourish and counterfeits will be less desirable. Once you are filled up, go and tell the good news to others to testify to what God has done in your life and set others free, just like this Samaritan woman did. Your story has the power to set others free!

Prayer

Lord, thank You that You see me and know me fully. Thank You that You offer me living water that never runs dry. Forgive me for the times I keep returning to empty wells that can never satisfy my soul. Help me to choose You today and every day as my source of true life, freedom, and joy. Fill me with Your Spirit and remind me that everything I need is found in You alone. In Jesus' name, amen.

Reflection Questions

1. How have you seen God go out of His way for you before? Recall a specific story that made you feel seen by God.

2. Who in your life needs to hear the good news of Jesus too? Write that person's name down and commit to praying for them and eventually sharing the hope of Jesus with them.

Day 7

Jesus, the Grower of Seeds

Reading: John 4:29–53

Key Verse: "Already the one who reaps is receiving wages and gathering fruit for eternal life, so that sower and reaper may rejoice together. [. . .] I sent you to reap that for which you did not labor. Others have labored, and you have entered into their labor." —John 4:36, 38

I'm not much of a gardener—in fact, I can't seem to keep plants alive for long. I've tried, trust me. I've tried watering schedules, plant food, moving them to better sunlight—you name it. Still, they usually wither away. Thankfully, God didn't call me to be a professional gardener. But even without a green thumb, I've learned one thing about plants: Growth takes time. Seeds don't sprout overnight. They need water, light, nourishment, and consistency before you see visible change.

In today's reading from John 4, Jesus uses this simple yet powerful image of sowing, reaping, and harvest to teach us something about sharing the gospel. He tells His disciples that sowing and reaping in God's kingdom works much like gardening. Someone has to plant the seed, someone else may water it, and eventually, a harvest comes. But the various segments of work aren't always done by the same person.

Pause and Reflect

Maybe you grew up hearing about Jesus but didn't truly believe until years later. Perhaps you had a single life-changing encounter with Him that opened your eyes to His love. Who planted the seed of the gospel in your heart? Who watered it? Did it happen instantly or over time?

For me, I grew up in a Christian household. I knew about Jesus, went to church, and understood the basics of the faith. But it wasn't until I was twenty-five years old that I fully surrendered my life to Him. Looking back, I see how my parents faithfully planted seeds in me—they prayed for me, taught me Scripture, and modeled faith in many ways in our home. Later, God sent a mentor who invested in me spiritually and challenged me to grow. My faith today is the harvest of their labor, the result of many seeds planted and watered over time.

This is what Jesus is talking about in John 4:36–38. The disciples are about to witness an incredible spiritual harvest in Samaria—not because they did all the work, but because others had already labored before them. Prophets, John the Baptist, even the Samaritan woman who shared her testimony—they all sowed seeds that prepared the ground. The disciples would simply step in and reap what was already growing.

The story of the Samaritan woman illustrates this truth so beautifully. One simple conversation with Jesus transformed her life. Instead of hiding, she ran to her town and said, "Come, see a man who told me everything I ever did. Could this be the Messiah?" (John 4:29 NIV).

Because of her testimony, many in her town believed. Jesus planted a seed in her, and she immediately became a sower herself—spreading the message and leading others to faith.

The disciples didn't plant these seeds. Yet Jesus tells them they will share in the joy of the harvest. This shows us that in God's kingdom, no effort for the gospel is wasted. One person plants, another waters, and someone else sees the final moment of transformation—but they all rejoice together because it's God who makes it grow.

As believers, this is our calling: to first know and abide in the One who saved us and to share that good news with others. Sometimes that means boldly sharing the gospel. Other times it's quieter—sending an encouraging text, offering to pray with someone, cooking a meal for a struggling friend, or simply listening to someone's pain. These may feel small, but they're seeds that God can use to bring eternal fruit.

Paul reminds us in 1 Corinthians 3:6–8:

> "I planted, Apollos watered, but God gave the growth. So neither he who plants nor he who waters is anything, but only God who gives the growth. He who plants and he who waters are one, and each will receive his wages according to his labor."

You may never see the full impact of a seed you plant. That co-worker you prayed for may come to Christ years later through someone else's words. A simple act of kindness may soften a heart that eventually responds to the gospel. You might not be there for the harvest, but your labor will not be in vain.

Sharing your faith can feel intimidating. Fear of rejection, awkwardness, or discomfort can keep us in fear. But never forget the Samaritan woman—she wasn't a trained evangelist. She didn't know all the answers. She simply shared what Jesus had done in her life, and God used it to change an entire town. Your testimony is powerful!

Your job isn't to save people—that's God's job. Your job is obedience: planting seeds when prompted and trusting that God will water them and bring growth in His perfect timing. Imagine the joy of one day standing in heaven, rejoicing with those whose lives were changed because you dared to plant a seed. That makes me teary-eyed imagining that.

Pause and Reflect

Who in your life might need encouragement, prayer, or a simple act of love this week? What does that act look like?

Today's passages challenge us to look around and ask: *Who in my life needs the hope of Jesus?* Maybe it's a friend, neighbor, or even a stranger God places in your path. Don't underestimate what God can do through a simple step of faith. Pray God would open your eyes and highlight someone every day to encourage.

Just as plants need good soil, pray that God prepares the hearts of those you speak to. Some seeds take root quickly; others take years. Your part is to scatter them generously and trust that God will do the rest.

Prayer

Lord, thank You for the people who planted seeds of faith in my life. Help me recognize the opportunities You give me to sow seeds in others. Give me boldness to share Your love without fear, and faith to trust that You bring the growth. May my obedience lead to an eternal harvest, where sowers and reapers rejoice together in Your presence. Amen.

Reflection Questions

1. What fears or excuses hold you back from sharing your faith with others?

2. What part of your testimony would you feel scared to share with someone? What would it look like to release that to the Lord and let Him use your story to bring someone else freedom?

Day 8

Jesus, the Healer of Sins

Reading: John 5:1–29

Key Verse: "When Jesus saw him lying there and knew that he had already been there a long time, he said to him, 'Do you want to be healed?' The sick man answered him, 'Sir, I have no one to put me into the pool when the water is stirred up, and while I am going another steps down before me.'" —John 5:6–7

When I was younger, I struggled with a habitual sin. I just kept going back to it over and over . . . It was years of secretly struggling with it, feeling shame and regret, yet repeating the cycle of this sin. Eventually, I became free of this sin by the power of the Holy Spirit. I was at a church camp, and the pastor on stage said, "If you are someone who is struggling with something and you want to be free, come down to the front." My heart began to race, I started sweating, and I looked around to see who might judge me if I were to go down to the front. Eventually, I thought to myself, *I'm sick of this sin . . . I want to be done with this.* I ran down to the front, not caring who would look at me, and full of tears and guilt, I confessed my sin to a leader at the front. That leader began to pray over me and tell me to say over and over to my sin, "You have no hold over me, in Jesus' name!" After that camp, I never went back to it. Did I still feel tempted by it? Yes, but I never went back. Jesus set me free from that sin! Thank you, Jesus!

Pause and Reflect

What's something that you are carrying that you need Jesus to set you free from? You might not be able to answer that right away, but pray about it and acknowledge it here.

Jesus is the healer of *all* sins, not just mine or yours, not just certain ones, but for everyone and all sins. In today's key verse, we see Jesus heal a man who had been lying on a mat for over thirty-eight years! That's a long time. We don't know why or how the man became paralyzed, but we do know that Jesus offered him the chance to be healed. Did you catch that? The man still had to *choose* whether he would take Jesus up on His offer and stand up or stay where he was.

Just like Jesus offers this man the option to be healed, He offers the same to us. Maybe you are currently stuck in habitual sin, like I was—it could be gossip, lying, cussing, or jealousy. Jesus asks you the same thing: "Do you want to be healed?" Sin is something we can overcome through Christ! We don't need to believe the lie that "It'll always be this way." We may still face temptations, but Jesus will always give us the power through the Holy Spirit to resist it. The question is—Do *you* want to be free? Freedom begins when you acknowledge your sin and you stop trying to fix it alone.

This man probably had reasons and excuses for why he couldn't be free. Perhaps you've done the same. It's time, my friend, to release those heavy burdens and invite Jesus into the places that still ache. Jesus longs for your freedom, but you have to be willing to take the first step. The more you focus on your Savior and not the sin, the quicker you'll experience the freedom your soul has been craving. You can't do this on your own, and that's okay. That's why Jesus died on the cross for you.

Just like I had to confess my sin to someone, you may need to do the same. James 5:16 says, "Therefore confess your sins to each other and pray for each other so that you may be healed. The prayer of a righteous person is powerful and effective" (NIV).

This verse tells us that to find healing you need confession and prayer with a trusted friend, mentor, or parent. Admittance, confession, accountability, and abiding in the vine are the keys to staying free. Are you ready to be free? The Healer is waiting for you with arms wide open, with no shame or guilt, just healing freedom. Maybe today you can do what I once did, saying out loud to your sin, "You have no hold over me, in Jesus' name!"

Prayer

Jesus, I thank You that You are my healer—not only of sickness but of every sin that tries to hold me captive. Lord, I confess that there are areas of my life where I've been stuck, where shame or fear has kept me from fully stepping into the freedom you offer. Today, I choose to believe that You have power over every chain in my life. I invite You to heal what is broken, lift the burdens I've been carrying, and give me courage to walk away from anything that keeps me from You. Thank You for Your mercy, Your patience, and Your unfailing love. In Your name, amen.

Reflection Questions

1. When Jesus asks, "Do you want to be healed?" what is your honest answer? What excuses or fears might be holding you back from fully surrendering to Him?

2. Imagine your life completely free from this sin or struggle. What would that look like? How would it change your faith, your joy, and your relationships?

Day 9

Jesus, the Obedient Judge

Reading: John 5:25–47

Key Verse: "I can do nothing on my own. As I hear, I judge, and my judgment is just, because I seek not my own but the will of him who sent me."—John 5:30

I went through a breakup once in a relationship that I really thought was *it*. You know, *the one.* But then it suddenly ended. I was shocked. Heartbroken. Confused. And honestly, disappointed in God. *Why would God let this happen? I thought this was my person.* Yet God had other plans. I couldn't understand why. My ex was a good guy—godly, smart, good family—you get the point. He checked off all the boxes on my self-made list. But I remember when I could tell the relationship was shifting toward an unhealthy place. I prayed a simple prayer in church: "God, if you want this relationship to end, I trust you." And that day, my ex initiated the breakup. Crazy, huh? It's powerful what surrendering to God's will can do.

In John 5:30, Jesus speaks these words: "By myself I can do nothing" (NIV). Jesus was making a bold statement and showing His dependence on His Father. He was constantly communicating with Him and seeking His perfect will. This is a picture of what it means to abide. And Jesus did it perfectly. He didn't do anything without seeking the will of God. Does that surprise you? If Jesus sought the direction of His Father, how much more should we?

I think that sometimes it can be easy to forget that Jesus' dependence on the Father wasn't a sign of weakness. It was actually a sign of perfect unity and trust. His surrender wasn't passive or weak. It was truly powerful. Jesus listened, obeyed, and aligned Himself with the Father's heart at every turn, with every decision. Jesus was anchored right into the will of God. That gives us a model for decision-making that is steadier than our feelings or our personal preferences. When we pause long enough to ask God for direction, we are making a deliberate choice to walk the path Jesus walked. That is a path marked by peace, wisdom, and freedom from regret.

Pause and Reflect

Think about a time when you've barreled forward with a decision without seeking God's will first. How did that turn out?

Hey, I've barreled forward too. My hand is raised! Once I ended up purchasing a car without considering God's will or even the counsel of my parents or any wise people around me, and I sorely regretted it. The car caused me all sorts of problems. It also cost me way more money than I should have paid. If I had listened to Proverbs 11:14, where it states, "Where there is no guidance, a people falls, but in an abundance of counselors there is safety," I would have prevented myself from making an expensive mistake.

This is what I've learned: Life without God will always lead us astray. And the way we seek His perfect will is to abide in Him, to make Him the center of our lives, and to seek Him in prayer. Abiding slows us down long enough to hear His voice instead of reacting out of fear, insecurity, or urgency. Abiding also creates space for God to redirect us, protect us, or even withhold something we want. Because—let's face it—He sees what we cannot see. When we choose to submit our decisions to Him, big or small, we invite His wisdom into places where our own perspective falls short. That's where real transformation begins.

We may not always understand God's will, but He always has His best in mind for us. Jesus always surrendered to God's will, not only here in John 5:30, but up until the very end of His earthly life. Jesus said to the Father right before He endured the cross, "Yet not as I will, but as you will." This should *always* be our prayer—Lord, *Your* will be done. His will is perfect and always better than ours. You will find His will in His Word. God will entrust you with more of His personal will for your life as you follow His revealed will in His Word. Make sure that as you are making decisions and seeking for God's plan over your life that it always leads you back to Him. God's will is always to make us holier and to look more like Him. He wants the best for us. Will you seek His will today?

Prayer

Jesus, I surrender my plans to You. Teach me to desire Your will above my own. Thank You for showing me, through Your example, what it means to live in full dependence on the Father. Forgive me for the times I've rushed ahead without You or tried to control outcomes that weren't mine to hold. Help me trust that You see the bigger picture—that Your ways are higher, wiser, and always rooted in love. Let my heart echo Yours: "Not my will, but Yours be done." Amen.

Reflection Questions

1. Recall a time when surrendering your own plan led to an unexpected positive result. What did you learn about God's character through that?

2. Where in your life right now are you clinging to control instead of seeking God's will?

Day 10

Jesus, the Abundance Giver

Reading: John 6:1–35

Key Verse: "Jesus then took the loaves, and when he had given thanks, he distributed them to those who were seated. So also the fish, as much as they wanted." —John 6:11

I distinctly remember one moment when I was stressing out about my finances and the bills were stacking up higher and higher. The invoices kept coming, and I didn't have enough to cover them. I began to spiral—so much so that I was losing sleep over it. You know that feeling? It's the lie-awake-at-night-and-worry-like-it-will-fix-something feeling. And it's the absolute worst, isn't it? Out of pure anxiety, I finally got down on my hands and knees and asked God, "Can you please help me?" I realize now that this is something I should have done from the start, before my worries started spiraling out of control. But two days after that pleading prayer, I got a random check in the mail, which covered my bills. All of them! It was a refund from something I didn't even know I was going to receive. Talk about miracle mail!

This is who God is—our provider, Jehovah Jireh! He provides for us in our needs right when we need it. The name Jehovah Jireh first appears in Genesis 22 (in the King James Version), when God provides a ram in the thicket for sacrifice, in place of Abraham's son Isaac. Jehovah Jireh literally means "the Lord will provide," which is a reminder to us that God sees the need before we do and already has provision on the way. God isn't a magic genie who gives us three wishes, but He is someone who deeply cares about our needs and is capable of meeting them.

I want to acknowledge that sometimes the answer doesn't show up like a ram in the bushes, like it did for Abraham and Isaac, or in our mailbox in two days, like it did for me. Sometimes we pray really hard, but the provision looks different than we anticipated. Other times it comes slowly, or through people or opportunities we didn't see coming. And sometimes we are still waiting. If that's you, I see you. Your story isn't an exception to God's goodness. His provision can come in many different forms and different timelines. But He still is who He says He is, Jehovah Jireh.

In John 6:11, God provided food for these travelers in the story from today's passage. Not only did He provide food for them, but He provided more than enough for them. The key verse says the people received "as much as they wanted." There was an abundance of food. (We'll talk more about the concept of abundance when we explore John 10 together.)

Back to today's lesson: Jesus had just sat down for a needed rest when He saw the crowd headed His way. His disciples began to worry. *How in the world are we going to feed all of these people?* You can practically hear the worry in Philip's voice: "It would take more than half a year's wages to buy enough bread for each one to have a bite!" (v. 7 NIV). Have you ever felt that way too?

Pause and Reflect

When have you worried that you didn't have "enough"—enough food, enough money, enough influence, enough time, enough [you fill in the blank]? Go ahead and write down what that is for you.

Jesus is our perfect provider. He is this same God who can take something little and make it grow or multiply. Trust Him as your faithful and trusted provider. He is the Bread of Life and also provides us our daily bread. He owns everything in the world and has no lack. Everything is His to give, and He has no shortage. He doesn't play favorites on who to give to, but He gives to those who call upon His name.

Just like God provided for me, He can do the same thing for you—in whatever you are needing. James 1:17 says, "Every good and perfect gift is from above, coming down from the Father of the heavenly lights, who does not change like shifting shadows" (NIV). He's the perfect gift-giver, and He will give in the perfect timing and way.

If God can do that with a boy's lunch, just think what he can do with your faith, your bold yes, your willing heart, and your two open hands. God doesn't need much, just someone who believes He can do much with it. Do you trust Him to be your provider, your Jehovah Jireh, or will you continue to strive in your own strength?

Spoiler alert: Jesus already knows your needs and your lack, even before you tell Him. Even so, He just wants you to come to Him and bring Him your needs in faith, trusting that He has the solution you are looking for. When He gives to you, don't forget to give

Him thanks. Praise Him before and after the gift. Never let the gift replace the Giver.

Prayer

Lord, thank You that You see every need in my life before I even speak it. Help me release my grip on worry and instead place my trust fully in You. Teach me to bring my "loaves and fish"—whatever I have—to You, believing You can multiply it beyond what I imagine. Strengthen my faith to trust Your timing, Your ways, and Your heart for me. Thank you for being my Jehovah Jireh. Amen.

Reflection Questions

1. How have you seen God's provision for you in unexpected ways?

2. What "small" thing in your life right now could you surrender to God, trusting Him to multiply it?

Day 11

Jesus, the One with the Words of Eternal Life

Reading: John 6:36–71

Key Verse: "'You do not want to leave too, do you?' Jesus asked the Twelve. Simon Peter answered him, 'Lord, to whom shall we go? You have the words of eternal life.'"—John 6:67–68 NIV

Being a Christian in today's world isn't easy. The pressure to have all the right answers, the judgment from those who don't understand, and the expectation to appear perfect so you don't misrepresent your faith can feel overwhelming. One quick scroll through social media makes it clear—Christianity isn't exactly popular. The temptation to hide our faith is real, whether out of fear of criticism or the desire to maintain a certain image.

In college, I gave in to that temptation. I kept my faith quiet so I could live how I wanted and avoid accountability. But that choice didn't bode well for me in the end. The things I chased left me empty. As I got older, I realized what I had been searching for all along was Jesus. I had tried everything the world promised would satisfy, only to find it hollow. Now, as a devoted follower of Christ, I know there is nowhere else to go. I've seen too much of His goodness, witnessed too many miracles, and found too much joy to ever turn back.

In today's story from the Gospel of John, we encounter people who walked closely with Jesus, witnessed His miracles, knew He was the Messiah, and yet *still* turned away from Him. The disciples also walked closely alongside Jesus and performed miracles with Him, but societal pressures and selfish desires tempted them to forsake their intimate and trustworthy relationship with Jesus. Ever done this too?

Pause and Reflect

Think of a time you might have turned away from God, despite seeing His goodness. How did that make you feel?

Yep, same. Many of us have been walking with Jesus for years and still get pulled toward the temptations of the world or shrink back when God calls us to stand firm. The longer I walk with Jesus the more that I know there is nowhere else to go to find the satisfaction I'm looking for.

At the same time, if you want to live a godly life, you *will* face persecution and trials for your faith, as the Bible tells us in 2 Timothy 3:12. It's not a matter of *if* but a matter of *when*. Don't let this scare you—because God will uphold you and reward you. But under pressure and persecution for your faith, will you stand for Him or step away from Him?

In John 6, Jesus performs one of His most well-known miracles—feeding the five thousand with just five loaves and two fish (a story told in all four Gospel accounts). The crowds are amazed, and many begin following Him, not because they truly understood who He was, but because they wanted more miracles and full stomachs. Jesus then begins teaching that *He* is the Bread of Life, the true source of eternal nourishment. But His words aren't easy to accept. He speaks of eating His flesh and drinking His blood, pointing to the deep, costly union of discipleship that would later be made clear through His death and resurrection.

But this was a hard and confusing teaching. For some, it was difficult to understand and even more difficult to follow. Many followers began grumbling, and in verse 66, we learn that some of his disciples stopped following Him altogether. Perhaps these followers wanted the miracles without the sacrifice. In verse 67, after many disciples turned away, Jesus looked at the Twelve and asked a piercing question: "You do not want to leave too, do you?"

Peter responded with words of deep loyalty and faith. "Lord, to whom shall we go? You have the words of eternal life." Peter recognized that there is nowhere else to go but Him.

Where in your life do you struggle with God's words and truths? How can you still remain faithful and echo Peter's words to Jesus, despite them being perhaps difficult?

There is nowhere else to go for joy, true life, and eternal salvation than Jesus. Everywhere else leads to a dead end. I've tried it and have fallen short every single time. You may falter and waver in your faith, but don't forget why you followed Jesus in the first place. God desires His followers to stay faithful, even under pressure and persecution. My prayer for you today is that you don't have to stumble into sin to find out that Jesus is the only place to go, and to discover that He truly is the only one with the words of eternal life. Jesus says to us in Matthew 10:32—"Whoever acknowledges me before others, I will also acknowledge before my Father in heaven" (NIV).

Jesus still asks this question of us today—"Do you want to go away as well?" The reality is, following Jesus will cost you something. You may lose relationships, opportunities, or approval. But you'll gain everything that truly matters—peace, joy, eternal life, and a relationship with the living God. He's worth going all in for and standing firm for His name. Will you stay or will you leave? There's nowhere else to find true life.

Prayer

Lord Jesus, You are the one with the words of eternal life. Forgive me for the times I've been tempted to hide my faith or follow the world's ways instead of Yours. Give me courage to stand firm when following You is costly, and give me strength to resist the pulls of this world. Help me remember that nothing else can satisfy my heart but You. When I am tempted to drift, draw me back to Your truth. Teach me to be faithful in every season, knowing that You are worth every sacrifice. In Your name, amen.

Reflection Questions

1. When have you felt the temptation to hide your faith or stay silent about Jesus? What held you back?

2. Think of a time when God's Word convicted you deeply. How did you respond—with obedience, resistance, or avoidance?

Day 12

Jesus, the Hated Truth-Teller

Reading: John 7:1–31

Key Verse: "The world cannot hate you, but it hates me because I testify about it that its works are evil." —John 7:7

When I first started my career in social media in 2010, I didn't post about Christianity or my faith at all. It was just secular, normal-girl types of beauty videos I made on YouTube. After going through a painful heartbreak, seeking counseling, and sitting alone with Jesus during the pandemic, He grabbed ahold of my heart, and my life began to change. I started to post and share more about my faith out of an abundance and overflow of what Jesus had done in my life. I couldn't help but talk about Him and how good He was, because He changed my life! To my surprise, I was met with a lot of negativity when my content changed. I would get comments like, "I didn't follow you for this religious content." "You've changed . . . I miss the old you." "You are so judgmental now." All because I was simply sharing what the Bible says and the truths that Scripture holds. Of course, this backlash was initially hard for me to handle, but I knew that Jesus' ways were true and right, even if others didn't agree with it. Truth hurts when it convicts you to change.

Pause and Reflect

Have you ever felt pushback or criticism simply for living out or speaking out about your faith? How did you respond?

Following Jesus means walking in truth—and the world won't always applaud that. Jesus himself was hated, not for doing wrong, but for boldly exposing darkness and hypocrisy. As His followers, we can expect resistance and criticism. Yet, this isn't a sign of failure—it's evidence that we belong to Him, stand for truth, and carry His light into a world that often prefers darkness. As Christians, we will face some persecution. We might even be hated for following Jesus (John 15:18). If you don't receive some backlash, you may need to ask yourself if you are standing for anything at all. In a world where compromise is encouraged, sin is celebrated, and pursuing the love of yourself is worshipped, be a person who is committed to fleeing from sin, relentlessly pursuing holiness, and dying to self. It's not about becoming holier than thou, but to be able to stand before the Lord one day and know you did everything you could to seek righteousness and purity for His name.

Jesus was hated and persecuted for telling the truth, not caving into societal pressures, and choosing to honor His Father. So much so that it brought Him to the cross. People didn't understand Him, nor did they try to understand Him. But Jesus knew who He was. He knew His mission. He didn't have to explain Himself, because He lived solely for the approval of His Father and not man.

Pause and Reflect

Where in your own life do you feel tempted to seek the approval of people more than the approval of God? Where in your life do you need to follow Jesus' example more and live for the Father's "well done" instead?

In today's reading, we spent time in John 7. This chapter takes place during the Feast of Tabernacles, when Jesus goes to Jerusalem and teaches openly. People are divided about who He is. Some believe He's good, others think He's misleading the crowd. The religious leaders grow increasingly hostile, even plotting to arrest Him, but His time had not yet come. Sadly, even His own brothers didn't believe in Him (v. 5.)

Today, we focus on John 7:7, where Jesus explains why the world hates Him: Because He tells the truth about its sin. "The world cannot hate you, but it hates me because I testify about it that its works are evil."

Jesus spoke with authority and courage, and He also exhibited great compassion. He healed the sick, lifted up the outcast, and welcomed people who were rejected by others. But He also boldly confronted hypocrisy and false religion, exposing the pride and corruption of powerful leaders. That's why He was so fiercely opposed. His light exposed the darkness, but not everybody loves light shining into the dark places. People sometimes feel safer in the dark—loving their sin or clinging to their pride. As followers of Jesus, we can expect opposition too. Yet we don't need to be afraid, because His Spirit strengthens us. His truth sets us free. And His love is greater than the world's hate.

Standing for truth, like Jesus, means holding both conviction and compassion. And when we do stand for truth, we aren't pointing to ourselves; we're pointing back to God, and His truth sets people free. Standing for truth and for His name doesn't mean you have to withdraw from everyone or point out every wrong. It means choosing to be a light in dark places and faithfully walking the harder road, even when it feels lonely. Following Jesus is the narrow path, and there may be moments when you look around and realize no one is walking with you. In those moments, take heart. God sees your obedience. He knows the cost, the tension, and the quiet courage it takes to honor Him. He upholds those who stand for Him, and He promises a reward that far outweighs temporary approval. One day, it will all be worth it. It is better to be hated for the truth than loved for a lie.

Prayer

Lord Jesus, thank You for being the perfect example of truth and courage. Even when the world hated You, You never wavered in living for the Father's approval. Help me to stand firm in Your truth with both conviction and compassion. When I feel pressure to compromise or seek the approval of others, remind me that Your "well done" is all that matters. Strengthen me to walk boldly in light, even when it costs me, knowing that You are with me and that one day it will all be worth it. Amen.

Reflection Questions

1. In what areas of your life do you feel most tempted to compromise truth for acceptance, and what would it look like to honor God instead?

2. Who needs to hear the truth of Jesus in your life? How can you share that more with them?

Day 13

Jesus, the Dividing Truth

Reading: John 7:32–53

Key Verse: "So there was division among the people over him." —John 7:43

When you think of Jesus, what words come to mind? Maybe you picture Him as safe, kind, loving, and full of grace. And He is. But we often forget that while Jesus is gentle and compassionate, His words and truth were also disruptive. The gospel is comforting, but it can also be divisive and even offensive, because Jesus radically challenged the way people lived and what they believed. While He often did it with much grace, He still spoke truth, even when it turned people away.

When I was younger, I remember asking, "Why would Jesus want to divide us?" after reading Matthew 10:34–37, where He says He will set people *against* each other. It's not that Jesus desires to pit people against each other, but it can be a result of following Christ. Jesus taught that God's kingdom is the "upside-down kingdom," with ways opposite of what the world values. The world says to chase and manifest money. Jesus says give abundantly and keep your life free from love of money, and be content with what you have (Hebrews 13:5). The world says you only live once, so party it up, but God says to lose your life to Him and serve Him. The world says to gossip and slander someone you don't like, but God says to pray for and forgive those who persecute you and make false accusations about you. The way of the cross is upside down, calling us not to preserve ourselves, but to die daily so we may truly live.

Pause and Reflect

Where have you fallen prey to what the world says is "good," only to find it wasn't? What did God desire for you instead, and what did you do about it?

The more you stand for His name and follow His plans, the more you might get pushback from friends and family who aren't following Him. In my life, I have distant relatives who have decided to no longer engage with my family because of this faith. This has been a long, disheartening journey for us, but we will never trade Jesus for the approval of man. Instead, we continue to pray for them, be a light, and hope God speaks to them.

While studying for this devotional, I found an author who sums up the offensive nature of the gospel in an eye-opening and challenging way:

"One of the most revolutionary actions of Jesus was also his most divisive. 'Now the tax collectors and sinners were all drawing near to hear him. And the Pharisees and the scribes grumbled, saying, "This man receives sinners and eats with them"' (Luke 15:1–2). The religious and political leaders during Jesus' day were upset that He was hanging out with the sinners—with the whores, the liars, the drunks, the democrats, the thieves, the financial extortionists, the republicans, the murderers, and so on. This is the divisive gospel of Jesus—that He would receive and eat with sinners. He eats with us.

"The message of Jesus is divisive because it goes against everything we have been taught, and everything we value. The ethic of the cross is counter-intuitive to our self-preservation, and yet, it is the only way forward in our Christian life. If we are to live, then we must die, continually, every day."* Amen to that!

Sometimes these words may be hard to hear, but know that the disciples too had a hard time with Jesus' words, as we can read in John 6:60. Jesus responds, "Do you take offense at this?" (v. 61). The gospel is offensive because it requires you to die to self and turn away from celebrating and accepting sin. Many people prefer to live in comfort and accept sin rather than turn away from it to choose the harder, yet more rewarding path of following Jesus. People want Jesus' blessings without sacrifice, salvation without dying to self. Many people believe in Jesus, but can you wholeheartedly and sacrificially follow Him? Following Jesus might feel difficult and scary in a world that glorifies sin, but it's always worth it. As the division in the crowd grew over the ministry of Jesus, He always remained true to the Father and offered them true life.

> On the last day of the feast, the great day, Jesus stood up and cried out, "If anyone thirsts, let him come to me and drink. Whoever believes in me, as the Scripture has said, 'Out of his heart will flow rivers of living water.'" (John 7:37–38)

Jesus knew their division and confusion was caused by their disbelief. But He also knew that what they truly needed was something only He could give them. And so He offered it time after time.

Times might have changed, but people haven't. People remain divided over Jesus and the Bible because they dislike truth and authority, and they don't believe in Him. It's a reminder that we are in a spiritual battle, not just a physical one. Satan hates when we stand for His name and make His name known. He will do anything to silence us and create further division.

When people dislike you for your faith, you don't always have to have the perfect answer. They might aim attacks at you, but you can show them love and grace, like Jesus did. Point them back to His Word. Jesus' heart isn't to purposefully bring conflict, but to bring people truth in order to set them free. He desires what's best for you, and that comes with rivers of living water flowing freely from His heart to yours.

Prayer

Jesus, thank You for being the truth that sets me free, even when it brings division. Give me courage to stand firm in faith and love those who don't understand or accept You. When I face rejection, remind me that You were also rejected yet never stopped loving. Fill me with Your living water so Your love flows through me, and help me choose obedience over approval every day. Amen.

Reflection Questions

1. Who in your life do you need to pray for who has disagreed with you about faith? What prayer specifically do they need from you today?

2. What in the Bible causes you to struggle with Jesus' words? What do you find offensive and hard to hear, yet you know it is the truth?

Day 14

Jesus, the True Freedom

Reading: John 8:1–38

Key Verse: "When Jesus spoke again to the people, he said, 'I am the light of the world. Whoever follows me will never walk in darkness, but will have the light of life.'"—John 8:12 NIV

Walking with Jesus in the light exposes the dark areas of your life that you may want nobody to ever see. I know this may feel scary and vulnerable, but His light isn't meant to harm you, but to heal you. At the beginning of this day's reading, the woman's sins were exposed, but this led to her healing. That's what light does—it reveals the areas of our lives that are still darkened by sin. Darkness in our lives can be a secret sin, like holding bitterness and resentment toward someone, perpetually lying about something to make yourself look better, or even unknowingly participating with something demonic. Darkness is everywhere. Take one look at Netflix and you'll see that the world loves darkness. Jesus called himself the Light of the World because He wanted everyone to know that He was the promised Messiah who had come to show us the way to the Father.

God has been leading His people with light since the beginning. Psalm 119:105 states, "Your word is a lamp to my feet, and a light to my path," meaning God's Word is a light to guide us every step of the way when we seek Him. When God led Israel out of Egypt, His presence appeared to them as a pillar of cloud by day and a pillar of fire by night to guide them (Exodus 13:21–22). That fire was His light leading His people through the wilderness. When the cloud moved, the people of God moved. When the pillar of fire stopped, the people of God rested. They couldn't always see what God was doing, but they knew where to look for His guidance. Sometimes He doesn't reveal everything right away, but you can trust that when you follow His Word daily, He *will* guide your path. It's one step at a time. If He were to reveal the whole plan, you might be tempted to try to redirect it, or you might feel like you no longer needed to depend on Him.

Pause and Reflect

In what area of your life do you need God's guidance right now? How can God's Word speak into your situation?

When you follow the Light of Jesus, it is going to be contrary to the world. The world's ways will lead you toward darkness. He will call you toward holiness and to "go and sin no more," like He spoke to the woman caught in adultery. But you can trust that wherever God leads you is always for your best. God does not want His children stuck in the darkness where there are shame, secrets, and hopelessness. Stay close to His light, because nothing grows and flourishes without it.

The closer you walk with Jesus, the more His light uncovers the hidden places in you that have yet to be brought into freedom. Jesus tells us, "If you love me, obey my commandments" (John 14:15 NLT). So, if you love Him and desire His light, invite Him into your darkness and trust that by surrendering your comfort, He will give you the freedom and relief you are looking for. And remember, we can't do this alone! Invite people into this healing as well.

When Jesus changes your life and changes you, people will noticeably see a difference in you. You will act differently, you'll smile wider, and you'll actually feel lighter. But you need an encounter with the Light first. Being a light starts with truly knowing and abiding in the Light.

Maybe there's an area in your life right now that feels heavy, dark, and dreary, or maybe there are hidden places you don't want anyone to ever see, ones that feel too broken or too scary to expose. The Light of the World has the power to heal anything. Don't let fear and comfort keep you from the freedom God deeply desires for you. Let today be the day that you expose everything into the light. You won't regret it. Your soul matters more than your comfort.

Prayer

God, I thank You that You are the Light when there is darkness all around me. Give me strength to follow You daily. Shine Your light on the areas of my life that need healing and meet me in my darkest places. Show me where I need to surrender more to You. Help me to feel Your light and bring it to others, encountering Your joy and presence each day. Thank You for being my constant source of hope and peace. Amen.

Reflection Questions

1. Where in your life right now do you feel you might be walking in darkness? Who can you bring into this situation so you can find freedom?

2. Recall a time in your life that God brought you out of darkness. What did you do to find that freedom? What will you do remain free in other areas of your life too?

Day 15

Jesus, the Freedom Giver

Reading: John 8:39–59

Key Verse: "So Jesus said to the Jews who had believed him, 'If you abide in my word, you are truly my disciples, and you will know the truth, and the truth will set you free.'"—John 8:31–32

Truth is something the world says is subjective. They say, "I'm living out *my truth*." Yet according to God's Word, there is only one truth and His name is Jesus (John 14:6). The world will tell you that everyone can have their own truth, but if that's legit, what's actually true if everyone has their own truth? We need one, absolute truth to have a foundation to go back to when things get confusing or disorganized. And when the world's "truth" is always evolving and changing, we should be grateful that we have God's unchanging Word. But what happens when we don't have the truth?

There was a time when I didn't know God's truth about me, and it caused me to act out in ways I wished I never did. In college, I went to the bars to seek validation from men and drink away my insecurities because I thought it would fix the hole in my heart. Once I met Jesus and believed what He said about me, I was able to replace all the lies I believed about myself and not go back to this detrimental lifestyle.

If we don't replace the lies with truth, we give power to insecurities, shame, and confusion to fester; the absence of truth will cause us to never walk fully in the victory Christ has for us.

The further our world gets away from God's truth, the more chaotic it gets. When we don't know God's truth—who He is and who He says we are—we leave a creaky door open to Satan. Satan hates freedom and truth because it goes against the very nature of who he is. Jesus tells us in verse 44 of today's passage that the devil is called the father of lies and that there is *no* truth in him. The enemy's strategy has never changed—he cannot create truth, only twist it. He offers lies dressed up as half-truths, taking what God has spoken and subtly distorting it to pull us back into darkness. It's no wonder our generation feels so confused; we've been persuaded to believe we don't need God, or that our way could somehow be better than His.

Falling into the thinking of "I can have *my truth* and a *little* of God's truth" is dangerous because it excuses sin and dismisses God's perfect plan for us, which is to live in holiness and righteousness for Him, not ourselves. I know you might be thinking, *I want to be able to do what I want and also still serve Him.* Friend, I wish that were the case, but that's not how it works in God's kingdom. Jesus tells the Jews that if they hold onto His teachings, they will be His disciples. Living for Jesus is denying your truth and choosing His truth, which ultimately brings you blessings. His truth isn't to bind you further or give you more religious tasks to follow, but to heal you and set you free. Jesus reminds us, "So if the Son sets you free, you will be free indeed" (8:36 NIV). When you know Jesus, He will set you free from whatever you may be facing today—whether that's habitual sin, anxiety, negative thoughts, self-harm, toxic relationships, or something else.

Pause and Reflect

What are some things you feel you need freedom from? These can be big or small. Write them here.

Jesus reminds His believers in this passage that if they abide in His words, they will know the truth, and it will set them free and show others they are truly his followers. Notice the chain reaction here: Abiding in Jesus leads to knowing the truth, which leads to freedom, and that freedom transforms you. And when you are truly changed, others can see that you are His disciple. Following Jesus is not meant to be passive. It's not just about filling your head with knowledge, but it's allowing His truth to penetrate your heart and reshape your life. Real discipleship doesn't happen by half-following His Word—it requires wholehearted devotion.

This devotional is called *The Abiding Way* for a reason. Abiding in Jesus isn't just visiting Him occasionally; it's dwelling in Him daily—for all the days of your life—while His presence changes you from the inside out. When you abide, you grow so close to Him that the temptations of the world lose their appeal. Abiding reveals truth about who He is and who you are, and it keeps you walking on the narrow path that leads to life.

My prayer for you today is that you would cling to His truth. His truth is what will free you from lies, heal your wounds, open your eyes to sin, and guide you for the rest of your life. Clinging to God's truth is essential in a world full of deception and distractions. Truth sometimes is painful, but it's what will set you free.

Prayer

Lord Jesus, thank You that You are the Truth that never changes. When the world is loud with confusion and lies, help me to cling to Your Word and abide in You daily. Set me free from anything that keeps me bound, and shape my heart to walk in Your truth with boldness and joy. In Jesus' name, amen.

Reflection Questions

1. What lies have you believed about yourself or about God that you need to replace today with the truth of His Word?

2. What is something you've been tempted to believe is "good" or desirable, even though it doesn't align with God's truth?

Day 16

Jesus, the One Who Heals Blind Eyes

Reading: John 9:1–25

Key Verse: "One thing I do know, that though I was blind, now I see." —John 9:25

On a visit to Alaska to see my sister, I met a Guatemalan woman (which was so cool since I'm half Guatemalan), and she shared her testimony of being blind and regaining her sight through the power of Jesus! I had never met someone whose sight had been restored before, but as soon as I read the story about Jesus healing a blind man, I thought of this amazing woman. Meeting her reminded me that Jesus still heals. These aren't simply stories from the Bible; these are stories for today. Jesus still heals not only spiritually, but physically too. As the body of Christ, we too have the power through Jesus to lay hands on the sick, blind, deaf, and paralyzed, and speak healing over their bodies. We do our part to pray and believe, and we leave the rest up to God.

In our reading today, we encounter a blind man who made the disciples curious. They wondered who bore "fault" for the blindness—the man himself or his parents. This would have been a common response at the time because of widely held beliefs that suffering was the result of some great sin. Jesus responded that this was not a sin issue, but rather the man was blind so that the work of God could be displayed through his life.

Then, Jesus did just that. He used this blind man's suffering to teach about faith and to bring attention to the power of God. Jesus put mud on the man's eyes and told him to wash in the Pool of Siloam. The blind man did as he was commanded, and he went home seeing!

Later, when questioned by religious leaders, the man said he didn't know how or why he was healed, he only knew that he *was*. "One thing I do know, that though I was blind, now I see" (v. 25).

What a powerful story. This story always brings to mind the topic of suffering and sickness. It is a mystery to me—and to many—why God heals some and not others. I don't have all the answers, but here's what I know: Sickness isn't God's punishment on you. He isn't sending cancer or the flu as payback for bad behavior. Sickness entered the world after the fall of Adam and Eve, and ever since then, creation has carried the weight of brokenness. As Christians, we don't have the ability to cure every illness, but we are called to bring heaven to earth. That means praying for healing, showing compassion, and remembering that God has given us authority to ask in the name of Jesus. He will do His part according to His will.

If you've ever doubted if God can still heal, remember: He's the same God today as He was in the pages of Scripture. That doesn't mean that every prayer will be answered the way we want. I've prayed my heart out for people who never got better. Yet I also know this: Sometimes God brings physical healing, sometimes He strengthens you through suffering, and sometimes the deeper work He's doing is spiritual healing that we will see in due time.

No matter what, His power and love remain constant.

Pause and Reflect

Maybe you don't have a physical or visual ailment, but one deep down inside that no one sees. Maybe it's something someone said to you years ago that you replay over and over, or the heartbreak you endured that still keeps you up at night. Maybe it's something someone did to you as a child that you still remember even when you don't want to.

Just as Jesus heals the blind, He wants to heal those places too that still cause pain.

Is there something in your life that still hurts when you think about it? Write it down. Invite God into it.

Jesus' healing isn't just for the physically impaired, but also for the ones who are emotionally and spiritually debilitated. Sometimes these wounds disable us in more than one way. They impair our relationships. They cause us to experience anxiety, fear, worry, and stress. They can adversely impact our ability to trust God, others, and even ourselves. If our hearts and minds stay sick, our spirits will too. When God heals you from the inside out, others can see the difference. Maybe you grow softer and gentler, less defensive and less driven to prove yourself to people. You steadily become a healthier, godlier version of yourself. Like the man in the story, you will be able to say, "I was blind and now I see." And your testimony will lead to others becoming free too. People will ask, "How were your eyes opened?" And like that man, you can give God all the glory. But we don't heal in isolation. We heal with vulnerability, transparency, and accountability.

Sometimes the enemy wants to keep us spiritually blind and cynical. He doesn't want us to believe God can still heal. The enemy will do anything to keep us impaired and locked up in lies, but know that nothing is too hard for our God!

Whatever you need today, go to God for it. Say it out loud—the thing that hurts the most to say. Jesus still heals. He goes to the deepest wounds and hurts in our lives and stitches them up. He's done that for me. I was once deeply blinded from seeing the truth of God, but now I *do* see.

I pray this increases your faith and your hope for whatever circumstances you're facing. God loves you too much to leave you hopeless and blind. He's the One who heals the blind, in every way possible. Open your heart to Him, and He will continue to open your eyes.

Prayer

Jesus, You are the One who opens blind eyes and heals broken hearts. Thank You for reminding me that Your healing power is not just something from the past, but it is alive and active today. I bring before You every wound, seen and unseen, and I ask You to touch the deepest parts of my life. Heal me where I've been hurt, restore what has been lost, and strengthen my faith to believe that nothing is too hard for You. Help me to walk in freedom and to share my testimony so that others may also come to see Your goodness. Amen.

Reflection Questions

1. In what areas of your life do you feel spiritually or emotionally "blind," and how can you invite Jesus into those places?

2. How does this story in John 9 encourage you to recognize healing—both physical and spiritual—as part of God's ongoing work in or around you today?

Day 17

Jesus, the One Who Gives Spiritual Sight

Reading: John 9:26–41

Key Verse: "Jesus said to them, 'If you were blind, you would have no guilt; but now that you say, 'We see,' your guilt remains.'"—John 9:41

When I was growing up, my dad used to say to me all the time, "Ignorance is bliss until it's not," when he wanted to warn me about dangers in the world that I preferred to ignore. I remember jokingly thinking, *Dad, stop . . . you're being annoying*. But looking back, he was right. Isn't it frustrating when your parents end up being right? Ignorance is something that you cannot be aware of until your eyes are opened to it. Once your eyes are opened, it's hard to unsee what you have now seen, unless you choose to look away. My dad reminded me of this when I listened to certain ungodly music. He could tell it was affecting my spirit, but I said it wasn't. Once I got older, I realized he was speaking truthfully to me, and I now no longer listen to the majority of music I used to jam out to.

In yesterday's devotion, we met the man who was blind and then received his sight through his encounter with Jesus. This miracle sparked intense controversy. Some people questioned whether Jesus truly had the power to heal, while the Pharisees—the religious leaders—objected because the miracle took place on the Sabbath. They considered Jesus' act of making mud and applying it to the man's eyes to be "work," something they believed was forbidden under the Law of Moses. Because Jesus didn't observe the Sabbath in the way they thought He should, many Pharisees concluded that He must be a sinner and therefore incapable of performing such a miracle. Many of them did not want to believe what they saw because it confronted and challenged their staunchly held beliefs. They saw the healing, witnessed the evidence, and yet still resisted believing that Jesus had done it. Believing a healing had truly taken place required them to admit who Jesus truly was: the Messiah. Much like the man was physically blind before he met Jesus, they were spiritually blind, unable or unwilling to recognize what was right in front of them.

This is still very much accurate today. People deny what they have seen, experienced, or heard because it will call them out of a lifestyle they want to cling to, or they are struggling with unbelief. Jesus asks this man, "Do you believe in the Son of Man?" And he says yes, allowing him the opportunity to go deeper with Jesus and worship Him. He had an encounter with Jesus that physically and spiritually healed him, despite the backlash he encountered. Jesus offers you the same question: "Will you fully believe me?"

Pause and Reflect

Has your testimony in or about the work of Jesus in your life caused people to question or doubt what He has done in your life? How did it make you feel? What did you say? Do you wish you had handled it differently?

I know in my life, once my eyes were opened to the gospel and God's goodness, it caused a reaction in me to change and confront my sin. Change is hard and also takes time. It didn't come overnight, but it was a gradual process of God consistently working on my heart and convicting me. Once you are shown the truth, it should cause a response out of you. The gospel should convict us and compel us to be sick of sin and things that break God's heart, but sometimes we may not feel ready to let it go yet—or part of us still feels comfortable in our sin. But once we become aware of what separates us from God, we should desire to remove anything that does so. Awareness of sin invites change and the ability of God to move in our life, but we have to want it. We have to be openhanded and openhearted to the Lord in order for Him to work in our lives. Unfortunately, the sin will catch up to you eventually. Ignorance isn't bliss. When we refuse to see or accept God's truth, we miss the blessings He wants to give us today and the spiritual growth He intends for our future.

God is inviting you deeper. His conviction doesn't come to condemn you, but to release you from the sin that distances you from Him and drains your joy. You still have a choice to receive His healing or to keep walking in blindness. Just like the man in John 9 who worshipped after his eyes were opened, my prayer is that you'll see God's goodness so clearly that it leads you to deeper devotion and trust. He is worth every sacrifice. Sin blurs our vision, but when God opens our eyes, He invites us into greater joy and deeper intimacy. And it's in that intimacy that you'll find a peace like no other. Trust me! Ignorance isn't bliss. Walking in God's presence is true bliss.

Prayer

Jesus, thank You for opening my eyes to Your truth. Forgive me for the times I've ignored Your conviction or stayed comfortable in sin. Show me where I need to surrender and give me courage to stand boldly for You. Expose anything that keeps me from Your light and fill me with Your peace and joy as I walk in truth. Amen.

Reflection Questions

1. In what area of your life has God opened your eyes to sin you might have been clinging to either now or in the past?

2. Will you stand boldly for Christ now that you have tasted His goodness? How will you do that in an everyday, practical way?

Day 18

Jesus, the Good Shepherd

Reading: John 10:1–21

Key Verse: "When he has brought out all his own, he goes on ahead of them, and his sheep follow him because they know his voice. But they will never follow a stranger; in fact, they will run away from him because they do not recognize a stranger's voice."—John 10:4–5 NIV

I come from a large family—nine of us in total, with me being the youngest of seven kids. Pretty wild, huh? Growing up was loud and chaotic, full of dishes and hand-me-downs and nonstop activity—but it was also so fun. Whenever we went to the grocery store, my parents had to load us all up and hope none of us got lost. One time, I did. I got separated in Sam's Club. I was terrified, convinced I'd never see my family again. Thankfully, my family had a unique whistle we all knew. Whenever we got separated, one of us would whistle, and instantly we'd know where to find one another. That simple sound has rescued me countless times. If anyone else tried whistling, it wouldn't fool me. I knew the sound of my own family.

That whistle reminds me of the voice of God. When you know His voice, other voices sound counterfeit. This is why John 10 is one of my favorite chapters in Scripture. It reminds us that God still speaks. His voice may not always be audible, but He is never truly silent. He longs to guide us, comfort us, and keep us from wandering in fear like I was in Sam's Club. In this chapter, Jesus compares us to sheep; sheep are trusting, defenseless wanderers and in need of a shepherd. Many of us are like this, wandering through life looking for purpose and direction, thinking we are intelligent enough to figure it all out on our own. But we are left defenseless and vulnerable to attack because we aren't relying on our Shepherd to help us. We were never meant to live apart from His direction. That's why Jesus calls Himself our Shepherd. He knows we are in need of protection and guidance. He declares, "I came that they may have life and have it abundantly" (v. 10). Yet many of us don't always feel like we're living that abundant life. *Where is it, God? Why does it seem absent?*

Pause and Reflect

Have you ever been lost? What were you thinking about when you couldn't find your way? What did you do? Did someone find you?

The abundance isn't found in fleeting pleasures or quick fixes, but in *abiding* with the Shepherd who gives it. Abundant life flows from staying close to Jesus and walking with Him daily. Nothing else can offer that kind of life. Jesus warns that the enemy comes only "to steal and kill and destroy" (v. 10). So if you feel destruction in your life, recognize where it is coming from. The enemy may try to win, but he does not have the final say, because we have power over him in Jesus' name!

The fullness of life Jesus offers is not found in occasional encounters with Him. It comes through daily surrender and continual fellowship. We were created for intimacy with Him, not for surface imitations. Resources like devotionals, podcasts, sermons, and books are wonderful tools, but they can never replace Jesus Himself. The only way to truly know His voice is to open His Word, pray, sit in His presence, and let His truth transform our hearts. As we study Scripture, His voice becomes unmistakable.

Think about designer-bag collectors. Over time, they become so familiar with every detail that spotting a counterfeit is easy. In the same way, when you immerse yourself in God's Word, you learn His voice so well that the enemy's lies stand out immediately. God's voice is always loving, gentle, and kind—never condemning, shaming, or manipulative. The enemy's whispers can never match the Shepherd's tone.

Jesus is called the Good Shepherd and the gate (vv. 11, 9 NIV) because a shepherd protects, guides, and cares for his flock—even at the risk of himself. He knows his sheep's needs and where they are susceptible to danger. Even when the sheep stray or make a mistake, the Shepherd always goes out of His way to bring them back home through the gate. Without the Shepherd guiding us, we will stray and rely on ourselves, leaving us vulnerable and isolated.

Sheep can't survive alone. A sheep without a flock is easy prey. Likewise, God designed us for intimacy with Him and for community with others. Maybe you've been struggling with isolation, convincing yourself you can handle life alone. This is your reminder: Ask your heavenly Father for a flock of believers to walk with you. Sometimes, discerning His voice is hard. That's why community matters. God places us in a flock so we don't walk alone. Other believers can remind us of truth when we feel tangled in lies. They help us discern when confusion sets in. Community won't replace God's voice, but it can confirm it and point you back when you're unsure. At the same time, never underestimate the Spirit's ability to speak directly to your heart. He can give you the wisdom and clarity you've been asking for, if you'll seek and wait on Him.

The Good Shepherd wants to guide you and speak to you, but will you let Him? He's a lot closer than you think. Press into Him daily with your whole heart and watch what happens. The abundant life He has for you starts with abiding in Him. Get so close to His heart and voice that nothing else will fool you. With the Good Shepherd, you'll discover the fullness your soul has always been searching for.

Prayer

Lord, thank You for being my Good Shepherd. Thank You for never stopping Your guidance, even when I wander. Teach me to know Your voice so clearly that no counterfeit can confuse me. Help me stay close to You through prayer, Your Word, and the community You've given me. Lead me into the abundant life You promise, and remind me daily that true safety and joy are only found in You. Amen.

Reflection Questions

1. What voices have been competing with God's voice in your life lately?

2. What is one practical step you can take this week to tune your ear more closely to Him?

Day 19

Jesus, the Protector of His Sheep

Reading: John 10:22–42

Key Verse: "My sheep hear my voice, and I know them, and they follow me. I give them eternal life, and they will never perish, and no one will snatch them out of my hand."—John 10:27–28

Recently I was doomscrolling social media and came across a video that pretty much sums up my life. In it, there is a sheep running for dear life through a pasture. When he comes to a large ditch, instead of leaping over it like the other sheep, he boldly dives headfirst into it. Thankfully, his shepherd is nearby and pulls him out by the wool of his neck. The sheep is so excited that he takes off again—only to leap straight back into the same ditch. The shepherd, unfazed, laughs it off and rescues him once again. This goes on not once but several times, which is probably why this video has gone viral. It's so funny! Some days, I keep my Good Shepherd pretty busy, just like this little sheep. Where would I be without Him?

Today's key verse really spoke to me because it reminded me of all the times in my life I've fallen into the ditch of sin and, unfortunately, repeated the same sin over and over. God has plainly and lovingly given us instruction in His Word to protect us from these very ditches that desperately try to pull us back in. If we truly followed His ways, we'd run far away from the temptations that keep calling our name.

A shepherd is always looking out for his sheep. The Bible says that all of us are like sheep who have gone astray (Isaiah 53:6)—or maybe like sheep who keep diving into ditches—because we are prone to wander. God's Word will always lead us toward protection. The fences or boundaries He places in His pasture are for our safety and security. God knows what it looks like outside of His green pastures—shame, guilt, regret, darkness, and addiction. But staying within His pasture, following His Word, is the safest place you can be.

You might have strayed—I know the feeling—but the Shepherd will leave the ninety-nine to pursue you. You, my friend, are worth being sought after. Everyone else may leave you, but the Shepherd goes after you to bring you back home. He wants intimacy with you, not just box-checking time with God. Intimacy with Him comes by slowing down long enough to hear His voice and recognize what it sounds like. He speaks through His Word, through worship, through other believers, through prayer, journaling, nature, and even the quiet prompting in your heart. The more you slow down to listen, the easier it becomes to hear Him. You will never hear His voice by going faster—only by going slower. His voice will always lead you back to His green pastures.

In John 10, Jesus was almost stoned after saying the words from today's verse. How could such a loving God be stoned for this? At the time, the Jews didn't understand that He truly was the Messiah. They didn't believe Him to be the one true Living God. Jesus tells them in verse 26 "But you do not believe because you are not among my sheep." Lack of belief in Jesus will prevent you from eternal life and the protection He desires for you. But He will never stop pursuing you. He does not want sin, the lust of this world, and the enemy's temptations to snatch you away. When you fully surrender to Him and believe that He is your Lord and Savior over your life, you'll never be snatched out of His loving hand.

Pause and Reflect

Take a moment to ask yourself what ditches you keep falling back into. Imagine yourself in His green pastures right now. What does that feel like? What are you free from?

Life on earth without His protection is just too hard, trust me. I tried it, and I never want to go back. To walk without the Shepherd is to wander aimlessly. To walk with the Shepherd is to be led and guided every step of the way with a spiritual covering. To know God is to know His voice and His commands for us, and then to follow them. On top of that, following His ways will never cause us to be put to shame, as Psalm 25:3 says. Following Jesus leads to true life—a life marked by purpose, joy, and His loving presence. He strengthens us and protects us, even in a world where suffering still exists. We will still face trials, but now we'll never face them alone.

We might ask ourselves, "This sounds easy in theory, but how do I *actually* do this?" It comes with time, spiritual discipline, and people helping us when we fall. Even the most devoted heart can drift when it tries to follow the Shepherd without the flock. Jesus had His disciples go in groups of two or three because He knew there is strength in numbers. Remember that the wolf attacks the sheep who has strayed from the flock. Don't believe that you are the anomaly who can survive alone. This life is so much richer with the King as your guide and friends along your side.

Take a moment to talk to your Good Shepherd who deeply wants to know you. He's one prayer away. Don't rush through this devotional without true connection with God. That's the whole goal of this book. Abide. Rest in Him. Seek His face. Pause right now and say this prayer with me.

Prayer

Father, I repent for my unbelief. Please show me if there is any unrepented sin in my life keeping me away from You and from hearing and knowing You. I want to hear You and follow You, but I need Your Holy Spirit to help me. Help me to not just rush through this book to check a box, but to intimately know You and abide in You. I love You. I need You. Speak to me and guide me. Amen.

Reflection Questions

1. When was the last time you did something when you knew it wasn't good for you? What did you learn from that?

2. If you could hear God's voice audibly right now, what do you wish He would say to you?

Day 20

Jesus, the Resurrection and the Life

Reading: John 11:1–27

Key Verse: "Lord, if you had been here, my brother would not have died." —John 11:21

Have you ever asked God to do something for you and He didn't? I asked God to keep a relationship together that I wanted so badly, yet it fell apart. Or when I prayed for my friend not to miscarry her baby, yet she still did. After the events, I always sit there and ask, "Why, God? You could have prevented this, but You didn't." Life with God is a constant juxtaposition between faith and surrender. It is your job to have faith in God's perfect plan and also to surrender your "perfect" plan, as hard as it may be. As Christians, we are faced with a decision of choosing to still follow God despite how He chooses to answer our prayers. There are many things on this earth that we may desperately seek answers for but never find. God is mysterious beyond our comprehension (Ecclesiastes 8:17). But I find comfort in knowing that I don't have all the answers, because if I did, I would be tempted to play God and make choices that don't honor Him. God is sovereign and has a perfect plan for everything, even when we don't understand.

In the story of Martha, Mary, and the death of their brother, Lazarus, Martha questioned Jesus' lack of promptness to answer her need. She wondered why Jesus didn't come sooner or heal him from afar, though He could have. Truthfully, Jesus could have raised Lazarus from a distance. It might even have been safer for Him to do so. Because of opposition from religious leaders, Judea was dangerous. Nevertheless, Jesus was willing to return there, despite warnings from His disciples. Martha may have begun to doubt, even though she had seen Him do miracles before. So often, this is us. We've seen Jesus work in our lives, but when He doesn't answer our prayer like we want Him to, we're quick to abandon Him. Once again, He went out of His way for His people.

Pause and Reflect

Do you remember a time when you prayed long and hard about something and felt like God delayed His answer? How did you feel? What did you do? Ultimately, what did you learn?

Perhaps God makes us wait for the promise or request to display His perfect timing and test our faith. Will we still follow Him even when the prayer goes unanswered? Jesus first delayed Martha's request and then fulfilled it, showing He works according to God's will, not man's. Through His actions, Jesus demonstrated that His delays were not denials. Just because it's not right now—or not at all—doesn't mean God is denying you. He isn't withholding from you. His ways are higher than our ways (Isaiah 55:9). Trials are often used to bring greater glory to God. The main mission of our lives is to give God glory for whatever miracles or answered prayers we do receive (John 11:4).

So why did Jesus wait? Some Jewish traditions taught that the soul stayed near the body for three days. By waiting until the fourth day, Jesus arrived when all natural hope was gone—making Lazarus's resurrection a clear and undeniable demonstration of God's power.

It may feel painful to never understand why God didn't answer at the time you needed Him, but sometimes God has us wait so that it is clear He alone was working. This story shows Jesus' empathy for us in the waiting and that His presence should be enough. Ultimately, Jesus and the gift of eternal life are what we should cling to most. Nothing on this earth is guaranteed, including our very life, but what we can cling to is this: When we trust in Jesus, He tells us that we will live even after dying. When we put our trust in Him, our souls will dwell with Him forever in heaven. It is easy to want answers here, but this world is not our home. Eternity should be our focus.

It's okay to doubt and wonder, *God, where are You*? Trust me, I've been there. I've been like Martha too, wondering why God didn't show up sooner. But let me remind you: God's delays are not His denials. Even when He doesn't answer in the way we prayed, He is still present, still working, and still good. He may not give us every "why," but He gives us Himself. Thankfully, Jesus does still answer prayers, as we see in this story. It may not always be immediate, but our job is to still come to Him and ask. Don't let one closed door make you close your heart to Him. Your doubts and questions are never too much for Him. And if the ache still lingers, listen closely to the story of Jesus in the readings for tomorrow.

Prayer

Father, I bring You my doubts, questions, and the moments I don't understand. Thank You that You aren't intimidated by my weakness but meet me with grace. Teach me to trust Your timing and rest in Your presence, knowing You are always working for Your glory and my good. Amen.

Reflection Questions

1. What unanswered prayer in your life has caused you to wrestle with God, and how might you begin to surrender it back to Him?

2. How can you remind yourself daily that God's presence is more valuable than the outcome you're waiting for?

Day 21

Jesus, the One Who Weeps with Us

Reading: John 11:28–57

Key Verse: "Jesus wept."—John 11:35

I have a dear friend who might be the most empathic person I know. Every time I've called her to share about a hard moment, she has gotten teary-eyed. If I cried, she cried with me. She's the kind of friend who will open up a bucket of ice cream, grab the tissues, and sit with you until you're okay. Sometimes you don't need someone to fix your problems but to just sit with you in them. Even if she knew the solution, she still would cry with me and hear me out. Raise your hand if you need a friend like this! We all do.

Thankfully, we have a friend like this in Jesus. He is the kind of friend who sits with us in our suffering. Jesus knows our life won't be void of pain, but He promises to give us comfort and hope. Hebrews 4:15 says, "For we do not have a high priest who is unable to empathize with our weakness" (NIV). He endured every kind of temptation and pain. So, when you think that God doesn't understand what you're going through, I promise you, He does.

Today, we read these two words: "Jesus wept" (John 11:35). If you were in a hurry during today's reading, it might have been easy to overlook this verse. After all, it is the shortest verse in the New Testament. Short, but powerful. It displays Jesus' heart and empathy. In yesterday's reading, we encountered Jesus having arrived after His friend Lazarus had died and already been in the tomb for four days. As the story continues, it's important to know that this story doesn't end at a tomb. It ends with revival. Jesus knew Lazarus would rise again, yet He *still* chose to sit with Mary and Martha and weep with them. John 11:33 says, "When Jesus saw her weeping, and the Jews who had come with her also weeping, he was *deeply* moved in his spirit and greatly *troubled*" (emphasis added). Let that sink in. Jesus knew the final result and that death wasn't the end of the story, but His heart just couldn't help but be moved for His people. It's who He is—compassionate and caring. Jesus didn't poke fun at them and say, "Why are you crying? Relax, I'm about to raise him from the dead!" He sat in their grief before displaying His glory through a death-to-life miracle.

Pause and Reflect

How does it impact you knowing that Jesus weeps with us, even when He knows the beautiful endings to our own stories?

I'm sure there have been moments when you cried and wondered if God cared. Let this be your reminder that God sees you. He is deeply moved. This life will always present us with grief, pain, and suffering, but in our weakness, God will make us strong. It's by His stripes and Word that we will find the strength to carry on (Isaiah 53:5). We are not supposed to carry our own burdens, because eventually they will become too heavy. Jesus tells us to cast our cares on Him (1 Peter 5:7) and that He will sustain us (Psalm 55:22).

When you feel weary or tired, call out to Him, the God who weeps with you. The God who says, "I am gentle and lowly in heart" (Matthew 11:29), meaning He is tender with you and not out of reach. I feel personally blessed to say there have been many times when I have felt so down and God has met me—whether it was by providing the exact verse I needed, a worship song that comforted my soul, or a friend who reached out because God knew I needed encouragement. Sometimes the pain is so real that all you can do is fall on your knees and weep, and that's okay. Mary did too. She fell at Jesus' feet and wept.

No matter what you go through, never forget this short but powerful verse: "Jesus wept." He knows that this will not break you and that He will sustain you. He knows a miracle can be done, and that grief is not forever. I know many people who have lost loved ones or gone through an insanely tough season, and the only thing that carried them through was the goodness of the Father and His people. Life is hard enough, so why suffer alone? Weakness is not failure. Vulnerability is strength.

As we pick up with Jesus' story, in verses 38–39, we see the rumblings of a miracle about to unfold: "Jesus, once more deeply moved, came to the tomb. It was a cave with a stone laid across the entrance" (NIV). Note here how Jesus not only gets emotional for them once, but *twice*. That really shows you His heart and character!

And here's where the story gets really good. With three words, Jesus summoned Lazarus. "Lazarus, come out!" (v. 43 NIV).

And that's what happened. Lazarus came out, alive.

That wasn't the only miracle that day. We learn in verse 45 that because of that long period of waiting that Mary and Martha endured, there was time for quite a crowd to gather as they supported Lazarus's loved ones in their grieving, and "many of the Jews, who had come to visit Mary, and had seen what Jesus did, believed in him" (NIV). Because Jesus didn't show up on anyone else's timeline, He could perform a miracle that resulted in a mass conversion of Jews!

Sometimes your miracle may come like that—a miracle where people get to witness the power of God, even though your waiting period felt unbearable for a time.

And yes . . . sometimes, this side of heaven, we don't get the miracle we ask for.

But even then, remember these two words: Jesus wept.

And He still weeps with us.

Even if you aren't in a tough season right now, you may need this reminder for the future—or for a friend who's hurting. Just as Jesus sits with us in our tears, be the kind of friend who sits with others in theirs. Be His hands and feet, and let others see His heart through you.

Prayer

Lord, thank You that You are a God who weeps with us. Thank You for showing compassion, tenderness, and care when our hearts are heavy. Help me remember that You are never distant from my pain but deeply moved by it. Give me courage to bring my tears and burdens to You instead of carrying them alone. Teach me to reflect your heart by sitting with others in their struggles and offering comfort the way You comfort me. Amen.

Reflection Questions

1. When was the last time you felt God's comfort in the middle of your pain, and how did He meet you there?

2. Who in your life might need you to sit with them, listen, and share the compassion of Jesus this week?

Day 22

Jesus, the Anointed King

Reading: John 12:1-26

Key Verse: "Mary therefore took a pound of expensive ointment made from pure nard, and anointed the feet of Jesus and wiped his feet with her hair. The house was filled with the fragrance of the perfume."—John 12:3

In today's featured story, set just six days before the Passover, we once again find Jesus with Mary of Bethany. Mary was known for her posture of devotion—she was the one who "sat at the Lord's feet listening to what He said" (Luke 10:39 NIV). It seems as though sitting at His feet had become her habit, the posture of a heart that longed to learn and love deeply.

Now, after Jesus has raised her brother Lazarus from the dead, Mary takes her familiar place once more—this time to anoint Jesus' feet. In that culture, a guest's feet were customarily washed with water and the head anointed with a small amount of oil or perfume. But Mary's act goes far beyond custom. She pours out a costly ointment on Jesus' feet and wipes them with her hair, an extravagant expression of worship and love. In doing so, Mary foreshadows what Jesus Himself will soon do at the Last Supper when He kneels to wash the disciples' feet, teaching his friends the way of humble, self-giving love.

Mary's act displays her utter devotion and love for Jesus. Following Jesus cost her something—public shame and an entire year's wage. But Mary knew that Jesus was worthy of it all. She could have kept a small portion of the perfume to herself out of fear or a scarcity mindset, but she didn't. She gave everything she had because she trusted the One who had already proven Himself faithful. She had seen Jesus perform miracles, so why would He fail her now?

Mary beautifully represents the kind of wholehearted worshippers we are called to be. At three different moments, she shows us what true devotion looks like:

In Luke 10:39, Mary sat at Jesus' feet and *learned*.

In John 11:32, Mary fell at Jesus' feet and *surrendered*.

In John 12:3, she anointed Jesus' feet and *honored* Him.

There's something about sitting at Jesus' feet that changes you. Sometimes it's all you can do when you've tried everything else. When you kneel before God—hands open and heart surrendered—you find the healing that no other posture can bring.

Mary did all this despite being mocked by Judas (who would later betray Jesus). Judas couldn't see the value of Jesus' presence over earthly possessions. To him, money mattered more than worship. Mary knew that money is replaceable, but Jesus is not. Jesus affirmed Mary's devotion, reminding both Mary and Judas that He would not be here much longer.

Mary's example encourages me deeply. Sometimes we overcomplicate what it means to meet with God, when in reality, it begins with simply sitting at His feet. But sitting at His feet often requires saying *no* to other things. One of the biggest distractions is right in our back pockets—our phones. They're quietly killing our intimacy with God. I am *so* guilty of it too. It's like the second I sit down to read His Word, little notifications start going off or I begin to think, *Hmm, I wonder what's happening on Instagram.* Anyone else?

Our sacrifice to know Jesus more may not look exactly like Mary's, but we still need to sacrifice something.

Pause and Reflect

Even now, following Jesus comes with a cost. Jesus may ask us to surrender a relationship, a job, the love of money, certain music, items keeping us in sin, or a selfish desire. You see, there is always a battle for our souls. Satan wants us to compromise and not fully go all in with God. He does not want us to sit at Jesus' feet, because he knows that is where freedom is found. In His presence, intimacy and healing are formed. The enemy will place people and things in front of us to keep us tempted, distracted, and entertained so that we never look to God for fulfillment. The result? We'll end up being half in and half out, like Judas.

Going all in with God is always going to be worth it, but it will require sacrifice. If we cannot surrender our comforts and sins, we miss the very freedom Jesus died to give us. He offered Himself willingly and lovingly, so that we could be made whole.

What is God calling you to sacrifice? What is something that keeps you distant or distracted from God? Write your answer below.

Sacrifice will likely look different for each of us. It might look like tithing extra one month even when your budget feels tight. It might mean distancing yourself from a friend who pulls you away from God. It might mean throwing away those steamy books you read at night that cause you to lust. It should cost you. Because if it doesn't, it might not be sacrifice at all. Jesus is worth the cost. In a world full of Judases who make fun of wholehearted devotion and don't see the value of true worship, be like Mary, who gave and loved and worshipped anyway. You'll never regret giving God your all physically and spiritually. You will be sowing seeds into your soul and into the kingdom that can never be taken from you.

Devotion for the Lord is never wasted. If your worship costs you nothing, it may be time to ask yourself, "Am I giving Jesus my all?"

Prayer

Lord Jesus, thank You for showing me through Mary's example what true devotion looks like. Help me sit at Your feet daily—not halfheartedly, but with my whole heart surrendered. Reveal what I need to sacrifice so nothing distracts me from intimacy with You. Teach me that You are worth more than any possession, comfort, or desire this world offers. May my life reflect worship that costs me something, because You gave everything for me. Amen.

Reflection Questions

1. What distraction will you remove to sit at Jesus' feet? How will you make this a habit in your life?

2. What about today's devotion challenged you in a way you haven't been challenged before?

Day 23

Jesus, the Unchanging One

Reading: John 12:27–50

Key Verse: "[. . .] for they loved the glory that comes from man more than the glory that comes from God."—John 12:43

When I moved to Los Angeles, I was twenty-five and ended up getting cast for a TV show. This show was supposed to be a reality/counseling show—confusing, right? They hired about twenty influencers and creators from different backgrounds and religions to give advice to someone struggling with a situation. In theory, it sounded great, but the real goal was to spark arguments and debates. *My least favorite thing.* I was the only Christian on the show, and they often picked on me to stir controversy. I sat there shaking, sweating, and panicking whenever they asked me to speak, because I wasn't that bold in my faith yet. Sometimes I even said things I didn't truly believe, out of fear of judgment. Thankfully, the show never aired because the plot was weak and confusing. But the whole time I thought, *I can't do this! What will they think of me?*

If you've fallen into the people-pleasing trap, you're not alone. We see evidence of it all over Scripture, as well as warnings for us to avoid it. God knows our temptation to please man over Him. Who doesn't want to be liked? But the praises of people are fleeting, and chasing praise is exhausting.

In our passage today, we see in verse 37 that "despite all the miraculous signs Jesus had done, most of the people still did not believe in him" (NLT). People had been encountering the miracles of Jesus, and we've read about many of them in our reading through the Gospel of John: Jesus turned water into wine at Cana (John 2). He healed the official's son (John 4). He fed the five thousand (John 6). He gave sight to the man born blind (John 9).

Even after all this, John tells us that some *did* believe, but they surprisingly remained quiet about it. As John 12:43 explains, "they loved the glory that comes from man more than the glory that comes from God." They were afraid of what the Pharisees would say, afraid of being put out of the synagogue, afraid of losing their status. The NIV translation says it this way: "[. . .] for they loved human praise more than praise from God." May that never be said of us.

Earlier in this chapter, the crowd shouted to Jesus, "Hosanna!"—a Hebrew word meaning "save us." Yet not long after, some of those same voices cried out, "Crucify Him!" Even though they had firsthand witnessed Jesus' power and healing, their loyalty shifted with circumstances.

So choose whose glory you want. Just as the crowd turned on Jesus, the applause of people can fade as quickly as it came, but the approval of God carries into eternity. Don't shrink back when it's time to stand. Stand firm, even if obedience costs you comfort, status, or acceptance. Cling to the Rock when the crowd leaves. Be faithful when it would be easier to blend in. Because in the end, it won't matter who clapped for you. It will matter that you stood for Him. And when you do, your quiet courage will point others not to your strength, but to Him who is within you.

Pause and Reflect

Do you relate to this—being more fearful of man than God? Share about a time that you feared man over God. How did that go?

Scripture warns us that living for approval is a trap. Proverbs 29:25 says, "Fear of man will prove to be a snare, but whoever trusts in the LORD is kept safe" (NIV). Fear of man keeps you bound. One day people love you, the next they won't. Especially in today's climate, many prefer to hear what they want instead of what's true. But you don't have to prove yourself to people if God is the only one you'll face one day. Show them the Light inside of you and let God handle the rest.

Paul put it bluntly in Galatians 1:10: "Am I now trying to win the approval of human beings, or of God? [. . .] If I were still trying to please people, I would not be a servant of Christ" (NIV). We cannot serve both man and God. Our mission on earth is to glorify Him, despite what people think. People will always have opinions, trust me, but only one matters. Though your hands may shake, His Word will not.

Jesus refused to live for the applause of people. In Matthew 12:38–39, the Pharisees demanded a sign to prove Himself. He refused, saying, "An evil and adulterous generation seeks for a sign, but no sign will be given to it except the sign of the prophet Jonah." He would not perform miracles just to satisfy critics. Later, during His crucifixion, He didn't try to prove who He was, because His identity was rooted in His Father. The same is true for you. Confidence in Christ replaces the pressure to perform.

Matthew 10:33 reminds us of the stakes: "But whoever denies me before men, I also will deny before my Father who is in heaven." God is looking for faithful people who will follow Him until the end, even when it's difficult. Looking back, I wish I could tell my twenty-five-year-old self that it's okay if people don't like you. Gently and boldly show them Jesus—that's enough. God will work on their hearts; you just need to keep yours focused on Him. A reminder I often need today still.

People-pleasing is hard to overcome, but it's worth fighting for. Unlike the shifting opinions of others, God's love and truth never change. Let His identity for you and love wash over you, giving people's opinions less power. Don't compromise truth to avoid rejection. Each time you choose His way over people-pleasing, you shine a light that points others to Christ and shows them where real security is found. Lean on the Rock; He will uphold you!

Prayer

Lord, help me keep my eyes fixed on You and not on the opinions of others. Give me courage to stand firm in my faith, even when it's uncomfortable. Remind me that Your approval is the only one that matters, and may my life point people back to You. Amen.

Reflection Questions

1. Where in your life are you tempted to still follow the crowds?

2. Who in your life could be encouraged by seeing you stay faithful, even under pressure? Who in your life inspires you to do this more?

Day 24

Jesus, the Servant King

Reading: John 13:1-20

Key Verse: "If I then, your Lord and Teacher, have washed your feet, you also ought to wash one another's feet."—John 13:14

We've all encountered someone who gets under our skin. Maybe it's a coworker, classmate, relative, or a casual acquaintance. The second that person speaks, you find yourself grinding your teeth and wanting to leave the room. It may even be the person you follow online—or don't follow because you can't stand them. You feel justified to gossip about them or curse them in your head because you find them irritating. Especially if they don't agree with you politically. Politics might be one of the most divisive forces in our society today. It often feels like the right hates the left and the left hates the right. But the truth is, Jesus would kneel to wash the feet of people on every side—just as He washed the feet of those who betrayed and denied Him. Jesus' love was never partisan, and His compassion never showed partiality.

In this part of John's Gospel, we see the servant heart of Jesus on full display. Chapters 1–12 highlight Jesus' public ministry—full of signs, teaching, and increasing rejection from many of the religious leaders and crowds. But in chapters 13–17, John shifts the lens. He zeroes in on the people who *did* receive Him. Jesus moves from public ministry to private ministry, focusing on those closest to Him.

In today's reading, on the night before His crucifixion, Jesus humbles himself to perform the task reserved for the lowest servant in the household by washing His disciples' feet. He always led by example, never telling His disciples to do something He hadn't done himself. He showed His disciples what obedience, humility, and love looked like in action. John tells us that Jesus removed His outer garment and knelt before His friends to wash their feet—a striking picture that foreshadows how His garments would soon be stripped from Him at crucifixion. This act of sacrificial love revealed the heart of the King above all kings. This was a kind of leadership no earthly ruler of His day would have demonstrated.

I imagine how shocking this would have been for the disciples, because this isn't something they would have deemed fit for Jesus. But He was teaching them an unforgettable lesson: Because of His deep *love* for them, He willingly chose to stoop low to serve them. Jesus always paired His words with actions. John writes that "He loved them to the end" (13:1 NIV), and here Jesus shows them one more time just how deeply He does. He does this even for Judas, who is about to betray Him, and Peter, who is about to deny Him. This is extremely convicting for me. How about you?

Pause and Reflect

How does your understanding of Jesus' love deepen when you remember that He served, loved, and even died for people who would betray and deny Him—and that He continues to love you with that same grace?

Think of all the people in your life who have done you wrong, talked bad about you behind your back, or done the unthinkable to you. Could you still wash their feet? Think of the people you may have hurt as well.

Washing someone's feet is a powerful symbol of forgiveness and servanthood. You may never literally wash someone's feet, but you can forgive them in your heart and serve them with your hands. When we speak of "washing feet," it's more than an outward, physical action, but it also points to the posture of our hearts. It's possible to serve someone all day long but still go to bed angry, resentful, and bitter. When we do that, it's not true foot washing. When bitterness takes root, the enemy gains dangerous ground in our hearts. Hatred is fertile soil for the enemy. That's why Scripture urges us to resolve conflict quickly, because God knows bitterness leads to resentment. We will always encounter people we dislike or disagree with, but following Jesus means learning to see them—and love them—the way He does. It will take His supernatural love to help you do this sometimes.

There was a case in Georgia where a woman named Regina Johnson tragically lost her husband of fifty years in a hit-and-run accident. The driver, Joseph Tillman, was under the influence. In the courtroom, Regina did something no one expected—she walked up to Joseph, hugged him, and said, "I forgive you, and God loves you." It was a moment that brought the entire courtroom to tears. Even the judge said he had never seen anything like it. When most people would have reacted with outrage, Regina responded with grace. In the face of unimaginable loss, she chose forgiveness over bitterness—and that kind of love can only come from God.

I urge you to both serve and forgive those who have hurt you. Forgiveness may not change the person who hurt you, but it will change you and set you free. At the same time, Jesus shows us that love is more than words. It looks like resisting to gossip about them, bringing them coffee on a bad day, and wishing well for them, even when the person doesn't seem to deserve it.

Imagine Jesus is sitting in the room, looking at that person next to you. What would He do? He'd show kindness, love, and grace—and then He would pick up the towel to wash their feet. There's a time and place for biblical rebuke and correction, but we often see this as Jesus' response first. But when we learn to see and serve people the way Jesus does, our hearts begin to soften. The enemy thrives on division and hate, but Jesus calls us to unity, love, and humble service. Don't give Satan a foothold through resentment or bitterness. It will poison your spirit long before it harms anyone else. To love and live like Jesus means laying down pride, picking up the towel, and revealing His heart to the world—not just to those who look like us or treat us well, but especially to those who don't. Loving like Him is the true test of our love for Him.

Prayer

Lord Jesus, thank You for showing us what true humility and forgiveness look like. You washed the feet of those who betrayed and denied You, and You laid down Your life for us while we were still sinners. Teach me to forgive as You forgive, to love as You love, and to see others through Your eyes. Remove resentment from my heart and replace it with Your peace and compassion. Help me to be an instrument of unity and grace in a divided world. Amen.

Reflection Questions

1. How might Jesus be inviting you to embody servanthood in your relationships this week—not just forgiving someone in your heart, but actively showing them love?

2. What's one simple, tangible way you can "pick up the towel" in your daily life at home, at work, or in your community?

Day 25

Jesus, the Example of Perfect Love

Reading: John 13:21-38

Key Verse: "By this all people will know that you are my disciples, if you have love for one another."—John 13:35

I once walked through a friendship breakup that left me deeply wounded. This was a friend I had known for years, yet our relationship suddenly crumbled over something small. On the surface it seemed petty, but in reality, it exposed deeper fractures in our friendship.

At the same time, I was growing in my faith while she was drifting from hers, and the gap between us became harder to ignore. What should have been a simple disagreement turned messy, pulling in mutual friends and leaving behind gossip, bitterness, and slander on both sides. I tried to make things right, but she wasn't interested in reconciling. The hurt left me wanting to fight back, to defend myself by tearing her down in front of our friends.

But then the Lord stopped me. He reminded me that most of those friends weren't believers, and that my reactions would either draw them closer to Christ or pull them further away. In that moment, I realized that every situation we walk through, even painful ones, is a chance to show others what it really looks like to follow Jesus.

Jesus told the disciples that the world would recognize them as His followers by their love. That's not something I've always done well. In Galatians 5:22, love is listed as the very first fruit of the Spirit because it's the foundation for everything else. Out of love flows joy, peace, patience, kindness, goodness, faithfulness, gentleness, and self-control. Jesus laid down His life because of His great *love* for us, the ultimate act of sacrifice and affection.

Love is hard to master because it requires humbling yourself enough to show grace, compassion, and kindness to people who may not look like you, think like you, or who have wronged you. But if Jesus could hang on a cross and pray for the forgiveness of the very ones who crucified Him, can we love and pray for the people who have hurt us—or even just the ones who get on our nerves?

Pause and Reflect

Is there someone in your life who's hard to love—but who still needs to experience the love of Jesus through you? How can you show that love or serve them this week?

Matthew 5:43–44, 46–47 says, "You have heard that it was said, 'Love your neighbor and hate your enemy.' But I tell you, love your enemies and pray for those who persecute you. [. . .] If you love those who love you, what reward will you get? Are not even the tax collectors doing that? And if you greet only your own people, what are you doing more than others? Do not even pagans do that?" (NIV).

I don't know about you, but these verses deeply convict me. It is so easy to love the people who like you, compliment you, make you feel good, and align with you spiritually or politically. But to love people who *don't* like you, curse you, or persecute you is a whole other level. Yet this is exactly the kind of love Jesus calls us to. His love isn't conditional. It doesn't stop when others mistreat, ignore, or even wound us. True Christlike love goes beyond comfort and convenience; it looks like praying for those who gossip about you, blessing those who curse you, and choosing forgiveness when bitterness feels easier.

This kind of love isn't something we can muster on our own. It takes the Spirit of God working in us to extend grace when everything in us wants revenge. When we do extend grace, the world sees something different—something holy. They see a reflection of Jesus Himself, who loved us even when we were still His enemies. The old saying "actions speak louder than words" is so applicable here. Even when everything inside of you wants to fight back, pray that the Holy Spirit will help you hold back and respond with love instead. Because this is how people will know we belong to Him. As Jesus said, they'll recognize us by our fruit—by the visible evidence of His love growing within us.

If we claim to follow Christ, then our actions must reflect the faith we profess. Our lives preach a louder sermon than our lips ever could. As I mentioned in my opening story, many friends were watching how I would respond to the slander and gossip, and while I didn't handle it perfectly, I still felt the Holy Spirit correct me whenever I got off course or did something I knew I shouldn't have. It's confusing to a nonbeliever when someone says they're a Christian but doesn't love like one.

I remember one specific moment when I prayed for the girl who hurt me. Even though it was extremely difficult, it was freeing! That's what fruit looks like. It's a byproduct of a faithful walk with Jesus. (We'll talk about this more on Day 28.)

Jesus modeled perfect love. He gave His life for the very people who spit on Him, beat Him, mocked Him, doubted Him, and ultimately ended up hanging Him on the cross. Remembering that truth humbles me and moves me toward compassion and grace for those who have hurt me or don't agree with me. With my job being online and posting about my life, I get a lot of hateful comments and opinions. It feels like a painful sting every single time, but I always try to remember that Jesus died for these very people.

First John 4:19 reminds us, "We love because He first loved us." We have the ability and power to love others through the love we first received from Jesus. We don't deserve this love, and yet He gives Himself unconditionally for us. This won't be the last time we hear Jesus command us to love one another, which tells us just how deeply He desires us to live it out.

God's love should change us. It should compel us to see others the way He does. We are only able to supernaturally love those who have wronged us because God has given us the power to do so through His Holy Spirit. I sure am thankful for His love because it has changed my life and the way I love others, and I pray it does the same for you.

Prayer

Lord, help me to love like You love. Show me who in my life needs Your love, even when it's hard. Fill me with your Spirit so my actions reflect your heart and point others to You. Thank You for first loving me and showing me what true love looks like. In Jesus' name, amen.

Reflection Questions

1. Who in your life is God asking you to love even though it feels difficult?

2. How might your response to conflict point others toward or away from Christ?

Day 26

Jesus, the Way, the Truth, and the Life

Reading: John 14:1-15

Key Verse: "I am the way, and the truth, and the life. No one comes to the Father except through me."—John 14:6

One time I was traveling to Los Angeles and was running so late to the airport that I was sprinting through the terminal, sweating and completely flustered. I finally arrived at what I thought was my gate only to have the attendant tell me, "You're at the wrong gate. This plane is going to Boston." *Sheesh, can a girl catch a break?* So off I went—running again—while hearing on the intercom, "Passenger Jeanine Amapola, please make your way to gate 5 before the door closes." I sprinted and slid in just in time. Phew! But imagine if the first attendant hadn't stopped me and just let me board for Boston. That wouldn't have been kind at all, right?

In today's reading, Jesus makes a powerful declaration: "I am the Way, the Truth, and the Life." Thomas asks Jesus, "Lord, we don't know where you are going, so how can we know the way?" (v. 5 NIV). Jesus lovingly removes all confusion by offering Himself—not a way, not one of many paths, but the Way. People today still need directions. They are often asking the big questions, like, "How do I get to heaven? What happens after I die?" Jesus answers clearly and compassionately—He is the *only* way to salvation. There is no other path.

Imagine if someone asked me, "Jeanine, how do I get into heaven?" and I replied, "Oh, pick whatever path you want; they all lead there somehow." That would be unloving. We live in a world that says all roads lead somewhere good. Pick your truth. Choose your vibe. Follow your heart. But if I had followed my instincts at the airport, I would've ended up one thousand miles off course. Spiritually, the stakes are even higher.

Jesus gives us one single path not out of exclusion, but out of kindness, to remove any wondering or guessing. God is not exclusive in His invitation. Scripture says, "Everyone who calls on the name of the Lord will be saved" (Romans 10:13 NIV).

Pause and Reflect

What keeps you tempted to board the "wrong" gate? What opened your eyes? What keeps you coming back to God's way?

To the world, the Jesus-only way can often feel aggressive and offensive because it seems to remove freedom of choice. But freedom to choose doesn't guarantee life. You can try every other god, but it will not bring eternal life in heaven with the one true living God. God's way isn't restrictive—it's protective. He knows all other paths end in confusion and death. Out of love, He gave us one clear way so we wouldn't be lost. If there were multiple ways, everyone would create their own version of salvation, which we already see in different religions today.

The Father's heart is not to exclude but to guide us into His loving truth. Jesus assures us there is room for us all in heaven: "My Father's house has many rooms; if that were not so, would I have told you that I am going there to prepare a place for you?" (John 14:2 NIV). His house is abundant, has many rooms, and He has prepared a place for you. He looked at you, saw you worthy of dying for, and loves you too much to withhold the Truth and the Way. But will you accept this Truth? Will you share that path with others who need it too?

Part of being a believer is helping to make heaven crowded. The best gift we can give is the gift of Jesus. He tells us, "Whoever believes in me will do the works I have been doing, and they will do even greater things than these . . ." (v. 12 NIV). This means the Holy Spirit equips us to share the gospel, heal, and stand boldly for Him. We don't become superior to Jesus; rather, His Spirit in us gives us the power to carry out God's will. Verse 13 reminds us that we can ask anything in His name and it will be done, not as a genie-style wish list, but so that God's will is accomplished and He receives the glory.

I came to know God more fully when I realized my own way wasn't working. I tried going to church occasionally and reading my Bible here and there, all the while still partying on weekends and thinking I could get by with good works. But I was anxious, confused, and empty. It wasn't until a mentor lovingly told me the truth that my heart softened. She helped me see that my way was leading me into darkness, while Jesus' way leads to peace and life. Her honesty, though hard to hear at first, changed everything for me. I'm forever grateful she gave me the truth instead of my DIY version of it. That's how we should all be with the people around us: loving them enough to tell them the truth, and telling the truth in a way that still feels like love. Think of it like pointing someone to the correct gate at the airport. You're helping them catch the right flight toward the right place.

I pray you never feel excluded by God. His invitation is always "Come as you are," and He promises to lovingly clean you up as you grow closer to Him. His arms are always open. All He asks is that you believe and let Him handle the rest. He welcomes you, prepares a place for you, and will lovingly guide you home whenever you wander.

Prayer

Lord Jesus, thank You for being the Way, the Truth, and the Life. Thank You that out of Your kindness, You gave us one clear path to salvation—not to restrict us, but to protect us. Help me walk confidently in Your way and not be distracted by the false paths this world offers. Give me boldness and love to share Your truth with others, even when it's hard. Remind me daily that You are preparing a place for me and that Your arms are always open. Amen.

Reflection Questions

1. In what areas of your life do you still try to follow "your way" instead of fully trusting Jesus as *the* Way?

2. Who in your life needs to hear about the true path to salvation, and how can you share it with both truth and love this week?

Day 27

Jesus, the Perfect Law Giver

Reading: John 14:15–31

Key Verse: "If you love me, keep my commandments."—John 14:15 NIV

One time, as a little girl, I accidentally watched a movie that had a nude scene in it, and it sparked a curiosity in me. I went online, searching for answers, and ended up seeing things I never should have seen. I carried this secret for so long that it held me in bondage. My dad was strict and often forbade us from watching certain shows because he didn't want us exposed to those very things. At the time, I was annoyed. I just wanted to watch them—*What was the big deal anyway?* But as I grew older, I realized my dad wasn't trying to boss me around or shelter me unnecessarily; he was protecting my young, innocent eyes. He loved me and wanted to shield me from the very thing that later kept me enslaved for years.

Our Heavenly Father is the same way. He wants to protect and shelter us from harm, evil, and sin, things that not only separate us from Him but also wound us deeply. He tells us to keep His commandments, not because His love depends on it, but because His commandments protect us. Without the revelation that His love is for our good, we may see Him as controlling, just as I once saw my dad. But once you understand the "why" behind His commandments, you begin to see why it's best to run as far from sin as possible. God's commands aren't arbitrary. Whether they refine us or protect us, they always flow from His love and are meant for our good—not our destruction.

In today's key verse, Jesus reminds us that if we love Him, we will keep His commands. But Jesus knew we could never do this alone. That's why, in the very next verse, He tells His disciples this: ". . . I will ask the Father, and he will give you another advocate to help you and be with you forever—the Spirit of truth. The world cannot accept him, because it neither sees him nor knows him. But you know him, for he lives with you and will be *in you*" (vv. 16–17, emphasis added).

Did you catch that? The Spirit dwells in us! That's how we keep His commands!

The truth is, when our main focus is to follow His commands, we end up striving in our own strength as we follow Him, and when we do that, we miss relational intimacy with Jesus. We make faith transactional, when it's not. When you fall in love with Him, obedience becomes the overflow of that love. Jesus didn't just say, "Obey my commandments." He began with, "If you love me." Obedience should flow from love. We follow Him because we love Him and know He is worthy of following. If we miss that love and adoration, our faith can slip into performance or legalism. Following God should come out of adoration for Him, not obligation. This changes everything—at least it did for me.

Pause and Reflect

Do you struggle with striving in your own strength as you walk with Jesus? What step can you take today toward relational intimacy with Jesus to make faith less transactional?

In our own strength, it's impossible to find freedom and perfectly follow His commands. We need the guidance of the Holy Spirit. I once heard a pastor say when I was in high school, "The more you focus on Jesus, the easier it will be to stop sinning." That later became so true in my life. I found freedom not by obsessing over my sin, but by focusing on my Savior. As I drew closer to Jesus and read His Word, it convicted me and changed me. It wasn't by my own might but by His Holy Spirit working in me that it led me to naturally change.

As Jesus continues to talk to the disciples, He says, "Anyone who loves me will obey my teaching. My Father will love them, and we will come to them and make our home with them. Anyone who does not love me will not obey my teaching. These words you hear are not my own; they belong to the Father who sent me" (vv. 23–24).

Jesus reminds us here that love and obedience go hand in hand. When we love Him, we naturally desire to keep His Word. As we walk in obedience, God entrusts us with deeper wisdom and understanding of His heart. He invites us into a closer, more intimate relationship—one where He makes His home within us. But when we choose to live as though sin doesn't matter, we show that our hearts may not yet be fully surrendered to Him. True love for Jesus transforms our desires. The more we love Him, the more we long to obey Him. Abiding in Him will lead to greater obedience. And that will change everything. When you see His love as the foundation, His commands won't feel like chains, but like shelter. I pray you remember that always when you feel this Christian life feels too hard. Focus on His love—He only wants the best for you.

Prayer

Lord, thank You for loving me enough to set boundaries that protect me. Help me see Your commandments not as restrictions but as gifts of love. Teach me to love You so deeply that obedience flows naturally from my heart. When I'm tempted, remind me that true freedom is found in You alone. Guard my eyes, my mind, and my heart, and help me walk in Your ways out of love, not obligation. Amen.

Reflection Questions

1. How might your love for God change the way you view obedience in your daily life?

2. What keeps you from wanting to obey His commandments? Which one is the most difficult one for you to keep? Invite Him into it now.

Day 28

Jesus, the True Vine

Reading: John 15:1-17

Key Verse: "I am the vine; you are the branches. Whoever abides in me, and I in him, he it is that bears much fruit, for apart from me you can do nothing."—John 15:5

We've finally arrived at my favorite chapter in the entire Bible—the chapter that inspired this devotional. The word at the center of it all is *abide*, and it is truly revolutionary. In today's reading, Jesus describes Himself as the true vine. This imagery gives us a clear visualization of how we must remain in Christ at all times in order to bear fruit and experience the fullness of joy He promises.

To abide means to remain, to dwell, to stay. Jesus calls us to remain in Him in *all* that we do, because He alone provides the nourishment our souls need to truly live. Just as a branch cannot survive apart from the vine, neither can we thrive apart from Him. When we try to do this life apart from Him, we will wither, and there will be no lasting fruit.

Jesus said, "Apart from me, you can do nothing." This is a humbling reminder that we are completely dependent on Him and that we need constant connection with Him to flourish. If we long to experience the fruit of Galatians 5:22–23—love, joy, peace, patience, kindness, goodness, faithfulness, gentleness, self-control—we *must* abide in the vine.

When I finally understood what it truly meant to abide, everything changed. I realized I had been striving in my own strength to be a "good Christian." I was *doing* all the right things for God and yet still wondered, *Why don't I feel any closer to Him*? I had worn myself down performing for His approval. I had become discouraged and finally had to ask myself, *Have I truly been abiding?*

Do you ever feel worn out, discouraged, and distant from God? If so, it's time to ask yourself the same question. *Have I truly been abiding?* Abiding isn't just rushing through a quick devo, but truly seeking Him, talking to Him, and trusting Him with *everything* we do. Abiding is so much deeper than going through the motions. It's intimate. It's daily, even hourly. It's not just seeking Him when it's convenient or out of despair, but rather knowing Him as your friend and Father, the One you can't do life without.

My friend Sarah, whom I talked about in the intro, spoke this word—*abide*—over me. Sarah knew I was like Martha in the Bible, someone who rushed around and did a lot of things *for* God instead of doing things *with* God. She felt that God had given her this word for me to encourage me to just sit with Him, which I found so hard to do at the time. She once told me, "When spending time with Jesus, don't just do what you think you should do. Ask Him how He wants to spend time with you. Just sit in His presence with Him. No agenda." How beautiful is that?

It was something I struggled with so much until the Lord almost forced me to slow down. My soul and body became weary from overworking and performing. Abiding was the best thing I did. Instead of just reading my Bible to check the box, I would often just sit on my knees with instrumental worship on and pray out loud to God. I would ask Him to speak to me and teach me things. I would usually leave in tears, refreshed because Jesus had just washed me with His love and presence. Just like Sarah encouraged me, I'm going to encourage you: Sit with Him. Pray to Him. Wait on Him. Linger longer with Him. Don't rush away and try to do this all in your own strength. He is all you need.

Pause and Reflect

Take a few moments and speak with God. Tell Him what you need and what you love about Him. He loves spending time with you. Write down what God is speaking to you.

Part of abiding is the pruning process. In John 15:6, Jesus says that the Father cuts off every branch that doesn't bear fruit and prunes the ones that do so they'll become even more fruitful. God is so invested in your growth that He will lovingly remove anything that hinders it.

Pruning isn't easy. It can feel painful sometimes, but it is so necessary. In order for new, healthy fruit to grow, the unhealthy branches must go. Pruning is essential because there are times when we cling to people, material things, bad habits, sins, and secrets. If there's something standing in the way of holiness, God wants to deal with it. It is not out of punishment, but preparation for what God has for you.

If you find yourself tired or just needing a touch from God, I encourage you to sit with Him in silence for fifteen minutes. Set your phone aside and remove other distractions. I know that might be hard at first, but trust me, you'll find yourself wanting to linger longer when you feel His presence. Abiding isn't a one-time thing; it's a daily decision in *everything* you do.

I want to share some final encouragement—again from my friend Sarah. Here's how she describes abiding in her own life: "I think of my spending time with Jesus in two ways, but both are abiding. When you're in a relationship, like marriage, you have times when you are doing life *with* your spouse. You run errands, you do things around the house, you're communicating, and you're together. This looks more like side-by-side, everyday life. And then you have your alone time with each other when you go on a date, you have face-to-face intentional conversations, and intimate moments with each other. Both are abiding. You're with each other in both scenarios, and both types of abiding are important as you build a close and loving relationship.

"Sometimes people just spend time with Jesus during their 'quiet time' and forget to commune with Him throughout the day. But when you're working, running errands, on the go, doing a project, you can stop and acknowledge His presence. Worship Him. Talk with Him. Tell Him how you love Him. Remain in what I call 'continual communion' with your Creator."

Sarah's encouragement definitely speaks to me as someone who still struggles to slow down. But remember this: The faster you move, the harder it is to hear Him. I pray that from here on out, you will choose to abide in Him and stay connected to Him in everything you do. He alone is the source of your nourishment. Nothing and no one else can replace or replicate Him.

Prayer

Lord Jesus, thank You for being the true vine. Teach me what it means to truly abide in You. Help me rest instead of strive, listen instead of rush, and stay connected to You in everything I do. Prune whatever keeps me from bearing fruit. Fill me with Your Spirit so my life reflects Your character and love. May I remain in You always. Amen.

Reflection Questions

1. What fruit from Galatians 5:22–23—love, joy, peace, patience, kindness, goodness, faithfulness, gentleness, self-control—do you need more of? Where in your life do you struggle to show this fruit?

2. How can you create more space in your daily routine to truly abide with Jesus?

Day 29

Jesus, the Innocent King

Reading: John 15:18–27

Key Verse: "If the world hates you, know that it has hated me before it hated you."—John 15:18

I'm not much of a crime-show girl, because I don't typically like filling my mind with that type of stuff, but I once watched a documentary called *The Innocence Files*. It follows several cases of people who were wrongfully charged with crimes, and it was heartbreaking to watch because many of them spent years in prison for something they never did. Watching their stories reminded me of Jesus, the truly innocent Savior and King who was put on trial and condemned even though He was completely innocent.

He was opposed by the religious leaders—the Pharisees, Sadducees, and scribes—because He threatened their traditions, exposed their hypocrisy, and undermined their authority. Political leaders like Herod and the Roman officials were unsettled by His growing influence, and they feared rebellion. And many in the crowds eventually turned away when they realized He wasn't going to be the kind of Messiah they wanted. When Jesus didn't meet their expectations, and when fear of the religious leaders grew louder than their faith, their loyalty proved shallow.

Jesus was no stranger to hatred or mockery. Yet, in His grace, He prepared us with the words from today's key verse to guide and comfort us when we face opposition for following Him. He didn't just warn us—He modeled how to respond to hate with truth, patience, and love. We may not face the level of backlash that Jesus did, but Scripture is clear that following Him can bring misunderstanding, pushback, and even rejection.

As an online Christian influencer, my DMs have been filled with hateful messages about my beliefs for years. I remember when I got that first message, it made me want to delete my account and never speak about my faith again. But what good is hiding the one thing that has changed my life? Why would I cave into the pressure of being silenced out of people-pleasing?

Jesus warns us about this because the closer we get to God and what His Word stands for, the more the world will hate us. I know that sounds scary, but if you are standing for His Word and getting hate for it, you're doing something right. It sounds counterintuitive, but God's ways aren't popular—not because they don't change lives, but because the world deems them judgmental, narrow-minded, and religious.

The Bible is clear in 2 Timothy 3:12–13: "In fact, everyone who wants to live a godly life in Christ Jesus will be persecuted, while evildoers and impostors will go from bad to worse, deceiving and being deceived" (NIV). This isn't to frighten you or cause you to shrink back from your faith, but to remind you it's normal to have pushback. Believe it or not, persecution is actually a blessing. Jesus tells the crowds in the Sermon on the Mount, "Blessed are those who are persecuted because of righteousness, for theirs is the kingdom of heaven [. . .] Rejoice and be glad, because great is your reward in heaven, for in the same way they persecuted the prophets who were before you" (Matthew 5:10, 12 NIV). How can persecution be good? How can I rejoice in someone hating me? I've asked myself that too. It takes time, the power of the Holy Spirit to strengthen you, and a knowledge of what you are fighting for. Fight against what God hates and stand firm for what God loves.

Pause and Reflect

Read the words of Jesus from John 15:18–27. Why did the world hate Jesus so much? Why might it hate you? How will you take to heart the words He spoke so you can keep the right perspective if and when it happens?

Maybe you're the only Christian at your school, job, or neighborhood, and people make remarks about you or assumptions because of your faith. Show them the love of Jesus. Don't cater your beliefs to your surroundings. Jesus didn't. Sometimes you'll be unjustly hated simply because you carry the Spirit of God within you. People may not like the conviction His presence brings. But don't let intimidation silence you. God will give you the words to speak when you ask Him.

So what should we be pursuing as we abide in Him? Staying sober-minded, walking in purity, holiness, forgiveness, justice, and integrity. Avoiding gossip, lukewarm faith, and compromise. Exposing darkness and standing for truth, even when it's uncomfortable. God calls us out of the world to look different from it, so don't be surprised when opposition comes. The more you speak boldly and fight back against darkness, the more opposition you may face.

When the world rejects you for following Jesus, don't take it as failure, take it as confirmation. You're walking the same road your Savior walked. Every time you choose obedience over comfort, truth over popularity, and faith over fear, you declare that this world is not your home. Persecution doesn't mean God has left you; it means you're carrying His presence so powerfully that darkness notices. Stay bold. Stay grounded. And remember, one day every ounce of hate you endured will pale in comparison to the eternal joy that awaits you. Keep going, friend. Jesus is on your side and so proud of you.

Prayer

Lord, give me courage to stand firm when the world misunderstands or rejects me. Remind me that You were hated first and that I am never alone. Help me speak truth with grace, walk in love even when it's hard, and fix my eyes on the eternal reward You've promised. Amen.

Reflection Questions

1. What area of your life feels hardest to live differently from the world right now?

2. What fears or insecurities rise up in you when you face criticism for your faith?

Day 30

Jesus, the Spirit and Truth Giver

Reading: John 16:1–15

Key Verse: "When the Spirit of truth comes, he will guide you into all the truth, for he will not speak on his own authority, but whatever he hears he will speak, and he will declare to you the things that are to come."—John 16:13

Have you ever wondered if God was speaking to you, or if it was just your own thoughts? Same. It can be so frustrating trying to discern the voice of God in a noisy world and with a chaotic mind. I have so many thoughts throughout the day that it's hard to know if I'm hearing God, myself, or the enemy. But if I know anything about God's character (and hopefully you do too by now after reading this book), it's that He only speaks truth, and that's what draws you closer to Him and makes you look more like Him.

Jesus told His disciples that He was going away, and that His departure would actually be to their advantage. In the moment, they couldn't understand why or where He was going. How could it possibly be good for Jesus—the One whom they loved, the One the crowds followed, the One who brought healing and hope—to leave?

Jesus came to earth in the form of a man, which meant He chose to take on the limitations of a physical body, and as a result, He could only be in one place at a time. That's why the crowds followed Him everywhere they could. They wanted to be near Him. But Jesus told His disciples that His leaving would actually be the best thing for them. Why? Because when He returned to the Father, the Spirit of Truth would come. No longer would they need His physical presence to experience Him; they could encounter Him anywhere, anytime through the Holy Spirit. This truth applies to us too! We can access and experience Jesus anywhere. He's not confined to a building, a book, or a physical body.

Jesus said He would send the "Helper" to us, the Holy Spirit. The Holy Spirit convicts us and speaks to us. Remember in the opening day of this devotional when we talked about God being three in one? This is where that concept comes full circle. The Holy Spirit is part of the Trinity and is God Himself speaking to us. If you've entrusted your life to Jesus, you have access to the Holy Spirit 24/7 because He makes His home in your heart. Think of Him as your built-in best friend who's always on a call with you.

Sometimes you'll get a thought in your head and wonder, *Was that me or God?* Jesus said the Holy Spirit convicts us of sin and righteousness. So if a thought convicts you of sin or draws you toward holiness, that's God through the Holy Spirit gently nudging you back to Him. He is called the Spirit of Truth because He can only speak what is true. If what you're hearing is belittling, destructive, or leads you toward sin, it's not God. Jesus said in John 14 that He is the Truth, so when He speaks, He will only declare what is true, good, and aligned with His Word.

That is why knowing God's Word is so important. It helps us recognize the lies of the enemy. Satan is called the father of lies (as we saw in

John 8:44—see how it's all connecting?). When you hear something that doesn't sound like God's voice, it may be the enemy trying to deceive you. Knowing and meditating on Scripture helps you fight back. Even Jesus did this! In Luke 4, when Satan tempted Him in the wilderness, Jesus used Scripture to destroy every lie. If Jesus Himself relied on God's Word to resist the enemy, how much more do we need to fill our minds with it daily?

Pause and Reflect

What lies do you believe right now about yourself or God? What Scripture could combat those lies?

God speaks through His Word and through the Holy Spirit. As you go about your day, pay attention to your thoughts. In Philippians 4:8, Paul encourages us to think about what is true, honorable, just, pure, lovely, and praiseworthy. If your thoughts don't align with these things, they're not from God. His voice will always lead you, and others, back to Him.

If you're feeling less than, unwanted, or unworthy, let the Holy Spirit remind you who you are and whose you are. You belong to Jesus, you are precious to Him, and you are bought with a price. He loves you too much to let you wander in confusion. The Spirit of Truth will always guide you back to what glorifies Him. Declare that over yourself as He declares it over you.

Prayer

God, thank You for giving me the Holy Spirit to guide and speak to me. I pray my thoughts and words align with who You say I am. Speak to me and remind me always of Your truth. Give me a hunger for Your Word and discernment to know it's You speaking, not the enemy. I love You and thank You for who You are. Amen.

Reflection Questions

1. Have you ever heard the voice of God? If so, what did He sound like?

2. What do you need the Spirit of Truth to remind you of right now that would change your life?

Day 31

Jesus, the Comforter

Reading: John 16:16–33

Key Verse: "Truly, truly, I say to you, you will weep and lament, but the world will rejoice. You will be sorrowful, but your sorrow will turn into joy."—John 16:20

In 2021, I lost a friend. He was someone I had known since I was seven years old. When I heard that he had passed away, I felt broken, confused, angry, and in utter dismay. Tears rolled down my face as I sat there in pure disbelief. I spent months trying to unravel his passing and asking God why this happened. Photos would pop up, reminding me of him and of the memories we made together. Grief was an unfamiliar concept for me, until then. I had to cling to God's Word and hope through it all, because without it I was left only with despair.

Have you ever experienced something like this too? It can feel gut-wrenching and isolating because others may not understand. Grief comes in many forms and looks different for everyone, and unfortunately no one is immune. In this life we will experience sorrow, because God warned us we will. Pain and suffering are unavoidable in this broken world, but it doesn't mean that you have to suffer alone. God says He "heals the brokenhearted and binds up their wounds" in Psalm 147:3, and today's key verse reminds us that regardless of the pain, there's a light at the end of the tunnel with the hope of Jesus.

Jesus spoke these words of comfort from John 16:20 to His disciples as He prepared to leave them. After spending so much time together—teaching, walking alongside, and pouring into them—He knew His departure would leave them grieving His absence. Yet even in that sorrow, He wanted them to know that joy was coming. He would return for them one day and they would spend eternity with Him. He wanted them to know that no matter what, they could access the joy that the Holy Spirit made available for them. The same is true for us today. We may not physically walk with Jesus the way the disciples did, but His Spirit, the Comforter, lives in us too. That means even in the darkest valleys of grief, we are not left alone. He promises a peace that "surpasses all understanding" (Philippians 4:7) and the kind of comfort the world cannot replicate. The sorrow you carry does not have the final word.

Pause and Reflect

What grief or pain are you carrying right now that you need to lay at Jesus' feet? How has this pain caused you to view God?

Maybe your loss or pain has caused you to doubt God or feel angry toward Him. I want you to know that is okay and totally normal. I've been there too. But here's the truth: God can handle your doubts, your questions, and even your anger. These feelings are a natural part of the grieving process. Tell Him how you feel. Journal your innermost thoughts, ones that are just between you and God. It's important to name what you are feeling so you can work through it and not get stuck. Don't let the enemy deceive you into thinking that God is no longer good—or that He isn't with you, or that it's impossible for Him to redeem hard things you face. I know God can redeem our struggles because He has done it for me.

The disciples couldn't understand at the time how Jesus' death could possibly be good. But on the other side of the resurrection, they realized it was the greatest good. Their temporary sorrow led to eternal joy. Likewise, we may not see the full picture in our moments of grief, but God does. He sees beyond the moment into eternity. Revelation 21:4 gives us this beautiful promise: "He will wipe away every tear from their eyes, and death shall be no more, neither shall there be mourning, nor crying, nor pain anymore, for the former things have passed away." The hard things you face will not last forever, my friend, even though I know it feels like they will.

So if you are carrying grief today, whether it's the loss of someone you love, the loss of a dream, or the heaviness of suffering, let this encourage you: Jesus is your Comforter. He is close to you through His Holy Spirit. He understands your pain, because He Himself was "a man of sorrows, acquainted with grief" (Isaiah 53:3). He is not distant from your suffering; He has stepped into it with you. And one day, He will redeem it fully, and it will all make sense.

Until then, we cling to His words: "In this world you will have trouble. But take heart! I have overcome the world" (John 16:33 NIV). That's not just a nice phrase; it's the anchor of our hope. When everything else feels shaky or uncertain, your Father in Heaven is not. He is steady, present, and right there with you. You can trust Him with all your fears and feelings. Nothing is too big or too hard for Him. He sits with you today in your grief or suffering.

Prayer

Lord Jesus, thank You for being my Comforter. You know the pain of grief and the sting of loss. You know what it's like to weep, to feel sorrow, and to cry out in anguish. Thank You for reminding me that my sorrow will one day be turned into joy because You have overcome the world. When the weight feels unbearable, draw near to me and remind me of Your promises. Help me to trust that You are close to the brokenhearted and that You will bind up my wounds. Fill me with the peace of Your Spirit and the hope of eternity with You. Amen.

Reflection Questions

1. How has God shown Himself to be near to you in seasons of sorrow?

2. When grief or sorrow comes to you, what truth of today's devo will you cling to?

Day 32

Jesus, the Intercessor

Reading: John 17:1–15

Key Verse: "I pray for them. I am not praying for the world, but for those you have given me, for they are yours."—John 17:9 NIV

Well, friends, we only have a few more days together. Hasn't this been encouraging and reflective? In this passage, we see Jesus begin to step into the very purpose for which He came—to go to the cross and fulfill every prophecy spoken about the coming Messiah. In the book of Matthew, Jesus teaches His disciples how to pray through the Lord's Prayer. But here, we witness Jesus sitting in the Garden of Gethsemane having a more intimate moment: a prayer *from* Jesus *to* the Father. It's a sacred, heartfelt conversation, almost as if we're being invited to overhear a private exchange between the Son and the Father. What a privilege it is to listen in on Jesus' heart, love, and intercession on our behalf.

John 17 is a transitional marker of Jesus completing His earthly ministry and beginning His intercessory ministry for us. This is Jesus' prayer to the Father before His crucifixion. Why does Jesus need to intercede for us? This is so important to know because it's essential to the gospel. Before Jesus interceded for us at the cross, God used covenants (for example, with Noah, Abraham, and Moses), prophets (such as Samuel, Isaiah, Jeremiah, Ezekiel, Daniel, and others), priests, and sacrifices as temporary means to communicate, guide, and redeem His people. There was always a sacrifice required for the Israelites to be in right standing again with God.

Before Jesus came, people couldn't approach God directly because sin created a barrier that needed atonement, which means forgiveness. But when Jesus came, He became the perfect and final sacrifice. After He rose and returned to heaven, He took on the role of our intercessor—our communicator with God. Now, instead of needing anyone or anything to make amends for us, we can come straight to God through Jesus. He's the bridge and final mediator that connects us to the Father, constantly covering us with His grace, forgiving our sins, and defending us, like a defense lawyer on our behalf. Pretty cool, huh?

Pause and Reflect

Where in your life do you need Jesus to intercede for you right now?

It is important to note that Jesus is the *only* mediator between God and man. No one else, as 1 Timothy 2:5 states, "For there is one God, and there is one mediator also between God and men, the man Christ Jesus." If someone tries to lead you to believe that saints, crystals, necklaces, candles, or angels can do this, they are leading you astray. If these items could hold the power that Jesus does, it would mean the cross was pointless and what Jesus did wasn't enough.

So what does this mean for you? This should give you hope that you have the King of the Universe on your side fighting for you! Jesus asks the Father to "protect them by the power of your name, the name you gave me, so that they may be one as we are one" (John 17:11). If you fall back into sin, face temptation, endure spiritual warfare, or feel oppressed by the enemy, call upon the name of Jesus. There is power in His name to save, heal, restore, and protect. He hears the cries of His people (Psalm 34:17). Without Jesus interceding on our behalf, we would be just like the Israelites still—stuck in a hamster wheel of performance, trying to get it all "right" in our own strength to earn God's love and forgiveness.

I pray this gives you a deeper appreciation of what Jesus did for us. I know it does for me. Jesus wants to be united with you, but it requires this revelation becoming true for you in your life. And just as Jesus intercedes for us, we should intercede for others. When you pray for a friend walking through a hard season, a family member battling illness, or even someone who doesn't yet know Christ, you are stepping into that same ministry of intercession that Jesus models for us. What a beautiful invitation, that God not only listens to Jesus' prayers but also welcomes ours to join in. At the same time, you may not have the strength to fight for yourself, but that's when the prayers of Jesus and others can carry you.

As you reflect on this passage, remember that Jesus is always pleading for you before the Father (Hebrews 7:25). You are never left alone, never left unheard, and never left undefended. The enemy may try to attack and accuse you, but Jesus is always actively protecting you. How gracious and kind is He. Never forget this beautiful attribute of Jesus when you are facing a difficult season. He is our perfect mediator and intercessor who loves you more than you can even imagine. He prays for you!

Prayer

Father, thank You for sending Jesus to be my mediator and intercessor. Thank You that through Him, I have direct access to Your presence and don't have to rely on rituals or sacrifices to be made right with You. I am grateful that Jesus constantly pleads for me before Your throne and protects me when the enemy tries to attack or accuse. Teach me to trust in His power and rest in His finished work on the cross. Lord, help me also to carry others in prayer, following the example of Jesus. Strengthen me to intercede for those who are hurting, wandering, or in need of Your saving grace. Amen.

Reflection Questions

1. How does it impact your faith to know that Jesus is continually interceding for you before the Father?

2. Who is one person God is putting on your heart right now to intercede for this week?

Day 33

Jesus, the One Who Sanctifies

Reading: John 17:16–26

Key Verse: "And for their sake I consecrate myself, that they also may be sanctified in truth."—John 17:19

Growing up in a Christian household, I heard so many "church words"—*salvation, anointing, sacred, reverence, sovereign*—and honestly, I had no idea what most of them meant. It wasn't until I got older, did my own research, and began truly reading the Bible for myself that those words started to become real in my life. These words weren't just fancy church terms; they were God's design for me, for us. The more I studied, the hungrier I became for truth. I wanted to truly understand what God's Word meant for my life and for those I loved. Words like *sanctified* and *consecrated* used to mean nothing to me, but now they mean everything. My prayer is that you would come to understand and live out these truths too.

We are going to begin to scratch the surface of two: consecration and sanctification. Before Jesus left His disciples, He modeled something profound, a life completely *consecrated* and *sanctified* to God. To be consecrated means to be set apart and dedicated for God's purpose. Consecration is the beginning of being set apart; sanctification is the journey of transformation. Both mean belonging fully to God. Consecration is our dedication, and sanctification is God's ongoing work in us.

Being consecrated to God isn't just a "church word." It's actually a daily choice. It looks like waking up every morning and saying to the Father, "Direct my thoughts, words, and choices." Being consecrated shapes how we speak and serve. It influences how we respond to stressful situations, and how we honor God in the ordinary and unseen parts of our everyday lives. Sanctification, similarly, is more than a church word. The ongoing journey of sanctification helps us choose patience over irritation, generosity over hoarding, and self-control over impulse. In the process of sanctification, God steadily transforms us—not in one big dramatic moment, but in thousands of surrenders over a lifetime.

Pause and Reflect

What concepts have you come to understand as you have committed your life to Jesus? Are there still "church words" or ideas that feel confusing or unclear? To get your thoughts flowing, maybe it's concepts like holiness, surrender, repentance, justification, God's will, the fear of the Lord, or being led by the Spirit. It's okay to wonder about these things! Write down the terms or concepts you've heard but never fully understood. Which ones do you want to grow in this year?

When Jesus said in today's key verse "For their sake I consecrate myself," He was pointing to the cross, the ultimate act of dedication and obedience to the Father. His entire life, not just His death, was an offering of love and surrender. He spoke only what the Father told Him to say and did only what the Father told Him to do. Everything He did was for God's glory, even when it led to suffering. And this is what makes His example so powerful: Jesus doesn't ask us to walk a path He hasn't walked Himself. He knows the cost of surrender, the discomfort of obedience, and the beauty that comes from trusting the Father completely.

We are called to do the same, to be living sacrifices, letting our lives reflect His holiness (Romans 12:1). One of the hardest prayers to pray is, "Not my will, but yours, be done" (Luke 22:42). It means surrendering our plans and trusting that God's will is better. That kind of surrender isn't loss, it's freedom. When you let God define what is good, you stop striving to earn worth and start resting in the worth you already have in Him. Sanctification becomes less about trying harder and more about letting Him reshape you from the inside out. When your life is guided by the Creator of the universe, you're not missing out—you're winning! You have everything because you have the Almighty God on your side!

God's desire is never to harm you but to help you flourish (Jeremiah 29:11). Sanctification may feel uncomfortable at times, much like pruning, but it's how God shapes you to become more like Jesus. The Holy Spirit works in you to convict, cleanse, and transform your heart so that your life would reflect Him. Jesus' prayer was that we would be sanctified in truth, that we would live differently, love differently, and look different from the world around us. We can only do this with the knowledge and understanding of His truth. To be set apart is to know for what purpose and from what.

When I was younger, I didn't understand how we could ever be holy. *Isn't that only for God?* But being holy doesn't mean being perfect; it means being set apart. It's not about *self*-righteousness, but righteousness—being in right standing with God through Jesus. Though we still live in this world, we're not meant to mirror it. It's why Jesus asked the Father to protect us while we are still in the world. We are called to reflect Christ. Consecration means dedicating our time, talents, and heart to Him; sanctification means allowing His Spirit to change us through it all. And the more you walk with Him, the more you'll begin to notice subtle shifts—your desires changing, your reactions softening, your heart becoming more aligned with His. That is sanctification at work. When you give Him your whole heart, day after day, abiding in Him, He will make you into something far more beautiful than you could ever become on your own.

Prayer

Lord, thank You that You set Yourself apart for me. Teach me what it means to be truly consecrated, to give You my full heart and trust Your refining process. Sanctify me in Your truth. Remove anything in my life that keeps me from looking more like You. Help me to walk in holiness, humility, and love today. Amen.

Reflection Questions

1. What areas of your life might God be calling you to set apart for Him?

2. Where do you think you still need purifying in your life?

Day 34

Jesus, the Willing Sacrifice

Reading: John 18:1–27

Key Verse: "Shall I not drink the cup the Father has given me?"—John 18:11 NIV

We've now arrived at the part of John's Gospel where the story turns from the anguish of the garden to the chaotic moments of arrest and trial. It's painful to read, knowing that an innocent man is facing betrayal, denial, and condemnation, ultimately culminating with death on the cross.

Today's reading begins in a garden nestled among olive trees, a place identified in some of the Gospels as the Garden of Gethsemane. The Gospel of John doesn't linger on what happened in the opening scenes of the garden. It says only this: "[Jesus] went out with his disciples across the brook Kidron, where there was a garden, which he and his disciples entered" (v. 1). The other Gospels add more details—not because they contradict John, but because each writer highlights different parts of the same true story. Think of it like several eyewitnesses describing the same event. One may focus on the emotions, another on the dialogue spoken, another on the actions happening. None are wrong. But together, they give us a fuller and richer picture of what unfolded.

In the other Gospels, we see Jesus in the Garden of Gethsemane praying to the Father, saying:

> "My Father, if it be possible, let this cup pass from me; nevertheless, not as I will, but as you will." (Matthew 26:39)
>
> "Abba, Father, all things are possible for you. Remove this cup from me. Yet not what I will, but what you will." (Mark 14:36)
>
> "Father, if you are willing, remove this cup from me. Nevertheless, not my will, but yours, be done." (Luke 22:42)

The "cup" symbolizes the suffering and wrath of God that Jesus was about to endure on the cross, taking upon Himself humanity's sin and separation from the Father. Yet, Jesus finishes His prayer with, "Not my will, but yours, be done." Even in deep anguish, Jesus yielded to the Father's will and to the very purpose for which He came, as we see in today's key verse. In this moment, He shows us that following God's plan comes with a cost, but it is always worth it.

Jesus tells His disciples, "The spirit indeed is willing, but the flesh is weak" (Matthew 26:41). Jesus' human flesh may have dreaded what was to come, but His spirit remained steadfast because it was in complete alignment with the Father. His Father was His strength. I love this verse because it reminds us that Jesus understands our human struggle—the daily battle between spirit and flesh. Unlike us, He never gave into His flesh. He chose obedience, even when it hurt. He made daily sacrifices to honor His Father, even when those choices were hard, misunderstood, or criticized.

Pause and Reflect

When have you felt the tension between the Spirit's desire to obey God pushing up against your flesh's desire for comfort or control? What helps you surrender in those moments?

In Luke 22:42–44, we're told that Jesus was in such agony that He sweat drops of blood. This rare medical condition, called hematidrosis, can occur under extreme stress or fear, often when someone faces death or torture. Even before the cross, our Savior suffered deeply out of love for us. The weight of the world's sin, the anticipation of separation from the Father, and the pain He was about to bear all pressed down on Him. Yet He still said yes. That's what makes Jesus the willing, sacrificial King.

Imagine knowing you were about to be tortured and executed. Any one of us would try to find an escape or excuse, but Jesus didn't. He stayed in Gethsemane, a place Judas knew well, fully aware that it was where He'd be found (John 18:2). Jesus could have hidden. He could have summoned angels. He could have silenced His accusers. But instead, He waited. Why? Because His love for us outweighed His fear of suffering. He remained faithful to the Father's plan over His life, even until death. He even protected the disciples in the garden by stepping in front of them (John 18:4–9). This is something He does spiritually for us every day against the enemy, shielding us with His strength and love.

If you ever feel worthless, undesired, or forgotten, remember this moment. The Savior of the world chose you and steps out in front of you. In His final moments, He thought of you. He didn't want you to be eternally separated from your Father. He laid down His life so you could live. Your friends, family, or even spouse will fail you at times, but your Heavenly Father never will. God saw your life as so valuable that He sent His only Son to take your place. No one can match His love, His sacrifice, or His willingness to suffer for you.

I pray you feel the weight of this story and moment and know that Jesus didn't do this in vain, but for us. It's humbling, because I know I'm not worthy of His love, but He still chooses me. He'd do it again, even if it was just you on earth. I pray this deepens your love and gratitude for Him today.

Prayer

Jesus, thank You for willingly drinking the cup meant for me. Thank You for choosing obedience when it would have been easier to run. When my heart feels weak, help me remember that You understand the struggle between spirit and flesh. Strengthen my faith to follow You with the same surrender You showed in the garden. Amen.

Reflection Questions

1. What does Jesus' willingness to suffer tell you about how He sees you? Does this change the way you see yourself?

2. Describe how you feel about Jesus after reading this chapter. What do you want to say to Jesus now?

Day 35

Jesus, the One Who Takes Our Place

Reading: John 18:28–40

Key Verse: "They cried out again, 'Not this man, but Barabbas!' Now Barabbas was a robber."—John 18:40

Being the youngest of seven kids was extremely fun, and as you might imagine, there were plenty of fights, pranks, and moments of pure sibling chaos. One time I was jumping on the couch (even though I wasn't supposed to), and I did a flip that resulted in my mom's favorite lamp shattering on the floor. When she came running in, I panicked and blamed it on my sister. *Devious, I know.* She got in trouble, and for a short moment, it felt nice to get off the hook. But eventually my sister told the truth, and the guilt of what I had done ate me alive. Finally, I owned up to my wrongdoing and faced the consequence I deserved.

If you have siblings, you probably know that feeling—someone getting blamed for your mistake, or maybe you were the one who took the fall for something you didn't do. That memory always comes to mind when I read John 18, a pivotal story when Jesus is about to take the punishment for not just one sibling, but for all of humanity.

Pause and Reflect

Can you think of a time when you were clearly guilty of doing wrong, but you were able to either talk your way out of it or cast the blame on someone else? Or maybe the situation was reversed, and you were the one who took the blame for someone else's wrongdoing. How did that make you feel at the moment? What about later?

In this chapter, Jesus is brought before Pilate, accused of claiming to be "King of the Jews," a threat to Roman rule. At this time, Judea was under Roman control, and while the Jewish leaders had influence over religious and civil matters, only Rome ruled and could authorize the death penalty. Pilate (the Roman prefect over Judea) and King Herod, though normally at odds, became strangely united that day over the death of an innocent man. "And Herod and Pilate became friends with each other that very day, for before this they had been at enmity with each other" (Luke 23:12).

Both leaders found no guilt in Jesus, yet the crowds demanded His crucifixion. When Pilate went outside to greet the throngs of people who had gathered, he acknowledged that the Jews had a custom in which one prisoner should be released at the Passover.

He asked, "So do you want me to release to you the King of the Jews?" (John 18:39).

But they cried out for the release of Barabbas instead. In the book of John, Barabbas' crime is listed robbery (see verse 40 in today's reading). But the other Gospels add more texture and details about his crimes.

Mark 15:7 and Luke 23:19 both reveal that Barabbas was among insurrectionists who had committed the crime of murder.

And yet that's the man the crowds wanted to release instead of Jesus.

Think about that. The Savior of the World, who healed the sick, opened blind eyes, fed the multitudes, raised the dead, and did nothing but love was condemned and a known criminal went free.

And in that exchange, we see the gospel: We are Barabbas. We are the guilty ones set free while Jesus takes our place. He didn't deserve the punishment, yet He willingly bore it so we could be forgiven.

When I think about that, I'm humbled. Any pride or self-righteousness quickly fades when I remember that without Jesus, I would be eternally separated from God. I've heard many people say, "I think I'll go to heaven because I'm a good person." But Scripture is clear: "There is no one righteous, not even one" (Romans 3:10 NIV). Our goodness could never earn us heaven—it's only by what Jesus did for us on the cross. Romans 5:8 says, "but God shows his love for us in that while we were still sinners, Christ died for us." Even when we sinned and were depraved, Jesus loved us enough to still die.

In my story, I wrongly blamed my sister. But in Jesus' story, the opposite happened. He was completely innocent, yet He didn't protest or defend Himself. He willingly accepted the role of the spotless Lamb, fulfilling every prophecy (Isaiah 53:7) and choosing to bear the weight of our sin out of love.

Jesus wasn't forced into this—He chose it. For me. For you. For Barabbas. For every sinner who would ever call on His name. It's not by your own merit that you earn salvation and grace, but by what He did for you. I pray this helps you always give glory and gratitude to Him because He is worthy of it! Tell Him how thankful you are today.

Prayer

Jesus, my heart is filled with gratitude as I remember the sacrifice You made. Like Barabbas, I was the guilty one. I was set free. And You were the one who carried the weight of my sin without hesitation. Thank You for this incredible gift of love. Teach me to live each day aware of the ways that you rescued me then and continue to do so every day. Strip away any belief that I can save myself. Let my life reflect the love You've shown, and may my worship come out of a heart overwhelmed by Your love and sacrifice. Amen.

Reflection Questions

1. How does remembering that Jesus took your place on the cross change the way you approach Him today?

2. Is there any area of your life where you believe you can "earn" your way into heaven? If so, how do you display that belief? Does this chapter of John change your mind on that?

Day 36

Jesus, the Crucified Savior

Reading: John 19:1–30

Key Verse: "It is finished."—John 19:30

This chapter is one of the most important in all of Scripture for us to know and remember, because it lies at the very heart of the gospel. What happens here changes everything—it's the reason we have freedom, healing, salvation, deliverance, and a restored relationship with God. When Jesus said these powerful final words, they were not words of defeat, but of victory. Jesus was declaring that He had accomplished everything the Father sent Him to do. He was not a victim of the cross but a willing servant carrying out God's redemptive plan.

If you've ever seen the 2004 movie *The Passion of the Christ*, you have some visual idea of the shocking pain Jesus endured on the cross and in the hours leading up to the crucifixion. To truly grasp the weight of His words—"It is finished"— we must first understand the reality of His suffering. Jesus was flogged, a punishment so brutal that many victims died before ever reaching the cross (Matthew 27:26 NIV). The Roman flagrum was a whip made of leather strips embedded with pieces of bone and metal. Each lash tore into His back, shoulders, and legs, ripping flesh and muscle. The Bible doesn't tell us exactly how many times Jesus was struck, but Roman scourging had no set limit and was often far more severe than the Jewish standard of thirty-nine lashes.

At Golgotha, Jesus was nailed to the cross. Large iron spikes about five to seven inches long were driven through His wrists. His feet were then nailed to the upright beam, one on top of the other. Every breath became a struggle. Crucifixion caused suffocation—the victim has to push up on their nailed feet to inhale, tearing open the wounds again and again. As hours pass, the body cramps, dehydration sets in, and the heart and lungs fail from exhaustion.

Please let this sink in. This was the physical price of our salvation. I can't help but feel overcome with emotion when I picture it, because Jesus endured all of that for us. Our loving Savior suffered the most excruciating pain imaginable, willingly, so that we could live. He suffered so much that He became disfigured and unrecognizable (Isaiah 52:14).

Jesus was crucified between two criminals—one who mocked Him, saying, "If you are the King of the Jews, save yourself!" (Luke 23:37), and another who humbly asked, "Jesus, remember me when you come into your kingdom" (Luke 23:42). These two men represent the world's two responses to Jesus: rejection or repentance. Which one are you? I know I want to be someone who is known by Jesus and makes His name known.

The soldiers and the crowd demanded that Jesus prove He was the Son of God, but He didn't need to prove who He was. It reminds me of when Satan tempted Him in the wilderness in Luke 4:9, saying, "If you are the Son of God, throw yourself down." He knew His mission and God-given identity. Jesus never bowed to the pressure of Satan or man. From His first breath to His last, He remained faithful and obedient to His Father's will.

Even in the midst of unimaginable pain, Jesus thought only of others. He prayed, "Father, forgive them, for they know not what they do"

(Luke 23:34). Those words still resound for us today. There are still people today who mock, reject, and doubt Him—but Jesus' forgiveness extends even to them. Maybe you've wrestled with doubt too. His grace is for you too.

Pause and Reflect

Does this reminder of what Jesus did for us help you believe more than ever? Do you see Jesus differently?

Someone once asked me, "Why did Jesus have to die on a cross? Couldn't God have chosen a less painful way?" I believe it happened this way so that we could fully comprehend the magnitude of His love and sacrifice. If His sacrifice had been easy or painless, we might never fully appreciate or understand the depths of His devotion to us. Jesus gave His body as the ultimate sacrifice, enduring what no one else has or *ever* could, so that we might know the full measure of His love.

Don't rush past this story. Sit with it. Let the reality of His suffering sink in. Jesus not only died physically, He carried the emotional weight of the world on His shoulders so that we could be free from the weight of our sin. He *who knew no sin* became *sin for us* (2 Corinthians 5:21). "It is finished" wasn't just a statement about His death—it was a declaration of victory, of redemption completed, of sin defeated, for us!

Thankfully, this isn't where the story ends. Let's keep reading to see where it goes. But for now, praise Him for finishing what only He could.

Prayer

Jesus, thank You for the cross. Thank You for willingly enduring pain, humiliation, and death so that I could experience forgiveness, freedom, and eternal life. Help me never take Your sacrifice lightly. When I'm tempted to doubt Your love, remind me of the nails, the scars, and the words "It is finished." Let Your victory over sin become my daily source of strength, hope, and gratitude. Teach me to live a life worthy of Your sacrifice, one that reflects Your love and obedience even in suffering. Amen.

Reflection Questions

1. When you hear Jesus' final words, "It is finished," what do they mean to you personally?

2. Which of the two criminals on the cross do you relate to more—the one who mocked or the one who believed? Why?

Day 37

Jesus, the Buried King

Reading: John 19:31–42

Key Verse: "So they took the body of Jesus and bound it in linen cloths with the spices, as is the burial custom of the Jews."—John 19:40

Have you ever received a call with bad news that left you in agony, waiting to see what would happen next? Maybe it was a call from the hospital telling you that someone you love is in critical condition and might not make it. You pace back and forth, stunned, praying there's still hope. Or maybe you've lost a loved one and found yourself wrestling with God, asking, "Why, God? Why would You let this happen?" That ache of grief, uncertainty, and waiting is something the disciples knew all too well.

In today's reading from John, sorrow fills the air. Before Jesus' death, Luke 23:27 says, "And there followed him a great multitude of the people and of women who were mourning and lamenting for him." Imagine how those same people felt afterward. They didn't understand God's plan or why Jesus died. I can also picture the disciples hiding, fearing for their lives, and sitting together in disbelief and heartbreak. Their beloved teacher and friend—a man who taught them, encouraged them, changed their lives, showed them their capabilities, and loved them till the very end was no longer accessible. How could this happen? He now lay lifeless in a tomb. He didn't deserve this.

John's account highlights how Jesus' death fulfilled ancient prophecies. When the soldiers pierced His side, blood and water flowed out (John 19:34). This fulfilled the Scripture that says, "They will look on me, the one they have pierced" (Zechariah 12:10 NIV). It also pointed to something deeper—Jesus as the true source of cleansing and new life. John later writes in 1 John 5:6, "This is the one who came by water and blood—Jesus Christ" (NIV). His death wasn't random or accidental; it was the divine plan of redemption foretold long before. Every detail, from the piercing to the fact that none of His bones were broken, was part of God's perfect design. His blood is the reason we have redemption!

Pause and Reflect

After spending the last few weeks together in the book of John, getting to know Jesus, how does this scene impact you? What would it have been like for the close friends of Jesus to experience His public trial, crucifixion, death, and burial? What do you think they were feeling?

After Jesus' death, two unexpected figures step forward to care for the body of Jesus: Joseph of Arimathea, a secret follower of Jesus, and Nicodemus, the same man who once came to Jesus at night seeking truth (John 3:1–2). Together, they tenderly take Jesus' body, wrap it in linen with spices—an act of honor and devotion—and place Him in a new tomb nearby. Even in this dark moment, God is at work, moving hearts and fulfilling His promises.

Now Jesus lies in the tomb. Three long days of silence, grief, and waiting follow. The world feels heavy, uncertain. I imagine Mary, His mother, weeping in her home, replaying every memory, every miracle. She didn't know resurrection Sunday was coming. Mary sat in anguish, not knowing she would soon see her son alive again.

This tension between Jesus' death and resurrection is important to reflect on because it reminds us where we would be if He had never risen. What if He had remained in the tomb? There would be no healing from sin, no victory over death, no fulfilled prophecies—only eternal separation from God. It would mean Jesus was not who He claimed to be, and our faith would be empty. As Paul writes, "If Christ has not been raised, our preaching is useless and so is your faith" (1 Corinthians 15:14 NIV).

But we know this isn't the end of the story, it's only the beginning. Just as Mary and the disciples grieved and reflected, we should take time to pause and remember too.

Just like the disciples waited and wondered if they would have hope again, wait well, knowing that there is hope is on the horizon for all your pain, and His name is Jesus. Nothing is too hard for the Lord, and He is working all things together for your good. What feels lifeless today may be the very thing God is preparing to resurrect tomorrow. Jesus is coming back! Take heart!

Prayer

Lord, thank You for the sacrifice of Your Son and for the hope we have because of the empty tomb. Help me to pause and truly reflect on what Jesus' death means for my life. When I face moments of grief, uncertainty, or pain, remind me that You are still working behind the scenes. Show me what I may need to lay down and put to rest in my own tomb. Thank You that Your empty tomb is why I have a reason to sing. Amen.

Reflection Questions

1. How does knowing that without Jesus' resurrection we would be still bound in sin and separated from Christ help you gain a deeper appreciation of Jesus and His sacrifice for us?

2. What "tombs" in your life—hopeless situations or dead dreams—do you need to surrender to Jesus for resurrection?

Day 38

Jesus, the Risen Lord

Reading: John 20:1–31

Key Verse: "Then he said to Thomas, 'Put your finger here, and see my hands; and put out your hand, and place it in my side. Do not disbelieve, but believe.'"—John 20:27

Have you ever had a friend tell you a story that you refused to believe until you saw it with your own eyes? Maybe you have that one friend who always has something *wild* happen to them, and it almost sounds too absurd to be true. I have a friend like that. For some reason, she always ends up in the most unreal situations. In a similar way, this is how Thomas must have felt when he heard that Jesus had risen.

Thomas is often referred to as "Doubting Thomas" because he didn't believe in Jesus' resurrection until he saw Him with his own eyes. Honestly, I can understand that. It sounds like the most incredible and impossible event to ever happen. I know many people today who feel the same way. They struggle to believe that Jesus could have really died and risen again. There are countless skeptics who question the truth of this story, yet Christianity stands apart from every other religion. With hundreds of eyewitnesses, consistent Scripture written by over forty authors, fulfilled prophecies, and ongoing archaeological evidence, the Bible has accuracy and transformative power like no other.

Still, in today's world, there are many who doubt or even deny the legitimacy of the resurrection story.

Pause and Reflect

Is there any part of the Christian faith that you struggle to believe? What doubts do you have? Tell Jesus about them and ask Him to help you to believe.

After Jesus' resurrection, there were likely many who felt exactly as you do, and exactly as Thomas did—shocked, uncertain, or skeptical that Jesus could truly return healed and whole. Even people who saw Him face-to-face, who touched His nail-scarred hands, still doubted. If people struggled to believe *then*, how much more might people wrestle with belief today? Yet God, in His mercy, continues to reveal Himself to those who seek Him.

Jesus told Thomas, "Have you believed because you have seen me? Blessed are those who have not seen and yet have believed" (John 20:29). Wouldn't it be remarkable to have been Thomas? To have seen Jesus in this way? Maybe you've wished you could see Jesus face-to-face like Thomas did. But Jesus says that we are blessed even if we haven't seen Him and yet still believe. That's the definition of faith—believing in something without seeing it. This is central to our walk with God, that we trust His Word is true and without flaw, even when we have questions.

I love that Jesus spoke these words to Thomas because He knew there would be generations of people who would wrestle with doubt. In Mark 9:24, a desperate father cries out to Jesus, "I believe; help my unbelief!" That verse has been a lifeline for many people who want to believe but feel confused and unsure—like a modern-day Doubting Thomas. I love knowing that Mark 9:24 is a prayer we can all pray when faith feels hard and belief feels thin. The enemy wants to keep you trapped in fear—and he wants to shame you for having even a shred of doubt—but God welcomes your questions, just as Jesus welcomed Thomas' questions. Bring those questions to Him in prayer. Even more, invite a trusted friend to walk with you as you sort through them. John understood that people might have doubts, which is why he writes in 20:30–31 that he recorded these things so that you may believe and, by believing, gain life through His name.

For me, Jesus has completely changed my life. My testimony alone is proof of His power. That's something no skeptic can take away—your personal encounter with God. Use it. Share it. Your story can inspire someone else to believe. And honestly? Reminding yourself of your own personal testimony and of God's work in your life in the past can bolster your *own* belief in hard times. That's the power of remembrance!

Faith might be one of the hardest parts of this journey because sometimes you just want physical proof that Jesus is near—but hold tight. Hebrews 11:1 says, "Now faith is confidence in what we hope for and assurance about what we do not see" (NIV). Remember, Jesus calls you blessed when you trust Him despite what you see. He is with you. Cling to the truth we've repeated throughout this devotional: He will never leave you or forsake you (Hebrews 13:5). He is interceding for you and working in ways you may not yet see or feel.

Jesus is risen, and because of His resurrection, we can have new life and eternity with Him. By His stripes we are healed. Though the disciples physically saw Jesus, we will one day too. Until *that* day, I pray that you feel His presence in *this* day. He is risen, alive, and for you!

Prayer

Jesus, thank You that you are alive and that Your resurrection gives me healing and salvation. When I struggle with doubt, help me to trust in Your truth. Strengthen my faith when I cannot see You, and remind me that you are always working in my life. Help my unbelief, Lord. Help me worship You in spirit and in truth. Thank You for Your resurrection! Amen.

Reflection Questions

1. What do you think of Jesus' words to Thomas? Do you realize He is talking about you and me?

2. How has your personal testimony helped you or others believe in God?

Day 39

Jesus, the Guarded Giver

Reading: John 21:1–14

Key Verse: "He said to them, 'Cast the net on the right side of the boat, and you will find some.' So they cast it, and now they were not able to haul it in, because of the quantity of fish."—John 21:6

I have done full-time social media as my job since I was twenty years old. When I first started, I was willing to do anything to grow my page and find success. Eventually, I did reach some of the milestones I thought would satisfy me—followers, numbers, and opportunities—but deep down, I still felt unfulfilled. As I grew older, my content changed alongside my relationship with Jesus. I realized that even though my work looked "successful," I was striving in my own strength. I wasn't using my platform for God's glory. The work felt unsatisfying. I didn't depend on God to lead or bless what I was building. I was trying to do it all myself. I wanted the glory. No wonder it felt exhausting and empty.

Friends and family began encouraging me to surrender it all to the Lord. They reminded me that God didn't need my "hustle," He wanted my whole heart. So, I decided to trust Him with my work. And let me tell you—it changed everything. When I stopped forcing growth and caring only about numbers, and started partnering with God, the results were organic and more peaceful because I didn't care if I grew or didn't. Why? Because Jesus was already my prize. It was no longer about what *I* could make happen, but what *He* could. Working with the Lord is always better than working for yourself. It is so much more rewarding than you could imagine.

When I read John 21, I see much of Jesus' heart on display. The disciples had gone back to what was familiar—fishing—after the resurrection of Jesus. Maybe they didn't know what else to do. Maybe they were waiting for whatever was next. Maybe Peter, after denying Jesus, felt too ashamed to imagine anything other than stepping into his old vocation. These disciples fished all night but caught nothing. The dawn came. And that's when Jesus appeared on shore and told them to cast their nets on the right side of the boat.

The moment the nets filled, John recognized Jesus immediately: "It is the Lord!" (v. 7). This miracle wasn't primarily about the abundance of fish. It was about revealing Jesus and about reminding the disciples of the One who called them in the first place. It's an echo of Jesus' call to them from the beginning, when He asked them to follow Him, to become fishers of men.

But here's something else I love—there's also a beautiful principle tucked inside this story. When Jesus shows up, the difference is dramatic. Look to the nets for proof! The night before, the disciples had worked in their own strength and came up empty-handed. But under the direction of Jesus, the catch of fish was overwhelming.

And—*don't miss this*—the nets still somehow didn't break!

That detail amazes me. Jesus was demonstrating something important for them, and for us: God protects what He provides. When He provides, He also sustains. He doesn't just give in abundance. He guards what He gives!

On their own, the disciples caught nothing. But with Jesus, there was abundance. In the midst of that abundance, Jesus was reminding them that their mission wasn't to sink back into what was familiar or safe. He had a calling for them, and they would need to trust Him to step into it fully.

Pause and Reflect

When in your life has God provided something for you that only He could have given? Take a moment to give him gratitude for that now.

We spend so much of our lives striving—trying to make things happen, trying to hold everything together, trying to maintain what we think we earned. But striving leaves us anxious and empty. Surrender, on the other hand, leads to peace. When we receive something good, it's because God ordained it, not because we forced it. God's blessings don't come through burnout or manipulation; they come through obedience and trust.

This characteristic of God frees us from the pressure to perform. The Lord never runs out of resources. He's not limited or stingy. He's not blessing everyone else while overlooking you. The same Jesus who filled the disciples' nets is the same Jesus who fills our lives today. When something truly comes from God, you won't have to fight to keep it. What's from God will draw you closer to Him, so you will honor Him and give Him glory. He knows your needs and cares deeply for them. His provision won't lead you to burnout; it will lead you back to Him, to a place of deep security and peace, knowing He's got it all under control.

Maybe today you find yourself empty-handed like the disciples after a long night of effort with nothing to show for it. Maybe you've been trying to make something happen—a dream, a job, a relationship, a breakthrough. You've been casting your net over and over again, but it just feels like failure. If that's you, remember this: Jesus is still standing on the shore, calling out, "Cast your net on the right side." He knows where the fish are. He knows what you need and how to provide it. When you trust His direction and surrender your effort, He steps in with supernatural provision. God loves to show you His faithfulness and that every good and perfect gift is from above (James 1:17).

Next time you feel fearful you'll lose something God gave you, rest knowing that He protects what He provides. He knows exactly what you need, when you need it, and how to deliver it in a way that reminds you of who He is. Let Him be the prize first before you get the thing you are praying for and don't forget to give Him glory and continue to worship Him even when you get it. Never forget that Jesus is enough.

Prayer

Lord, thank You for being both my provider and my protector. Forgive me for the times I've tried to make things happen in my own strength instead of trusting You. Help me release control and surrender my plans into Your hands. Remind me that everything good comes from You and that You know what I need before I even ask. Teach me to rest in Your timing, Your wisdom, and Your faithfulness. May my work, dreams, and desires bring glory to Your name. Amen.

Reflection Questions

1. What are you striving for that you need to surrender to God?

2. Where do you need to let God provide?

Day 40

Jesus, the Perfecter of Our Faith

Reading: John 21:15–25

Key Verse: "The third time he said to him, 'Simon son of John, do you love me?' Peter was hurt because Jesus asked him the third time, 'Do you love me?' He said, 'Lord, you know all things; you know that I love you.' Jesus said, 'Feed my sheep.'"—John 21:17 NIV

We've made it to the final chapter—hurray! I am teary-eyed as I write this because this has been such an amazing journey with you. Even as I've written these pages, I've fallen more in love with Jesus myself. His Word is alive and active today, and it still has the power to transform us when we take time to read it, believe it, and live it out.

At the close of this Gospel, Jesus gives His disciples one final charge: Follow me and feed my sheep. After all they had seen, the disciples knew how to follow Jesus—not perfectly, but faithfully. They had walked beside Him for three years, watching how He honored the Father and loved people with humility and compassion.

After His resurrection, Jesus appeared to His disciples by the Sea of Galilee and had a conversation with Peter. Three times He asked,

"Do you love Me?" and three times Peter replied, "Yes, Lord, You know that I love You." Each time, Jesus answered, "Feed My sheep." Peter had denied Jesus three times, but here we see Jesus gently restoring Him, one question for each denial. Something Jesus will do over and over with us too. Jesus was showing Peter that love for God must overflow into love for others.

"Feed My sheep" means to care for, guide, and lead God's people to the Father with love and truth. I love that Jesus leaves His disciples with this, because it's what He did on earth. He's inviting us to continue His mission—to care for the lost, help the weary, and point people back to Him. We cannot truly love others until we first know His love. We cannot help set others free unless we've personally experienced the Truth that sets us free. Everything begins with a genuine relationship with the living God. My prayer is that through these forty days, you've come to know Him more deeply—that your thinking has been stretched, your vision of Him expanded, and any misconceptions unraveled. Isn't He amazing? Isn't He worthy? He is.

Pause and Reflect

How has reading this devotional helped you understand Jesus' character more clearly? How will that change how you live from here on out?

Throughout this devotional, we've watched Jesus radically change lives and disrupt culture's religiosity, heal the sick, set captives free, open blind eyes, cast out demons, and reveal the heart of the Father in everything He did. I love how John closes out this chapter to tell us in verse 25 that what we've read is only a *glimpse* of all Jesus has done. He performed so many miracles and touched so many lives that the whole world wouldn't have room for all the books written about Him. John ends the book on such an amazing note to attempt to have us grasp the impact Jesus had on the world. What we've read throughout this whole devotional is scratching the surface on all the amazing miracles Jesus performed and will continue to! I pray as we end on this final chapter of John that this helps you try to comprehend how much Jesus loves us and has a heart to help His people.

So as we end this forty-day journey, I leave you with this:

If you stumble along the way, remember that He is patient with you. Repent quickly. Confess your sins. Go to Him for everything. Seek His plan above your own, and talk to Him like a friend, because that's what friends do—they talk and hang out with each other. He longs to walk with you daily like He did with the disciples.

Next, feed His sheep. Don't keep this joy to yourself. Share the good news of what Jesus has shown you. Pass it on. Be bold in your faith. Help others experience the same hope you've found in Him, because free people set other people free, and people need the hope of Jesus. Some people are just waiting for someone to tell them they are loved and chosen, and that someone could be you.

And finally, *abide* in Him in all you do. With Him, you will bear fruit and find true life. The abundant life you're longing for isn't found in success, people, or possessions—it's found in knowing Him intimately and making Him known. When you feel fearful, weary, lonely, or scared, abide in Him even more. Surrender the need to have everything figured out and trust He does that for you. Give Him your time, attention, and heart.

I want to thank you for joining me on this forty-day journey through the Gospel of John. My prayer is that this isn't the end but the beginning of a lifelong pursuit of Jesus. I hope it has left you even more in love with Jesus than before. He loves you more than you know. Wherever life takes you, abide in Him. It will bless your life more than you can imagine.

Prayer

Jesus, thank You for these forty days spent in Your Word. As this journey ends, help me to keep walking closely with You every day. Help me follow You and share Your Word with others. Let the Holy Spirit change me to look more like You. Let what I've learned take root in my heart and bear lasting fruit. Teach me to love like You, live for You, and share Your truth with the world. You are worthy of all my praise, now and forever. Amen.

Reflection Questions

1. What aspect of Jesus' character stood out to you most throughout these forty days?

2. What will you do to stay rooted in Him?

Notes

Day 1 Jesus, the Living Word of God

* Blue Letter Bible. "Lexicon :: Strong's G3056—λόγος." Blue Letter Bible. Accessed December 10, 2025. https://www.blueletterbible.org/lexicon/g3056/kjv/tr/0-1/

Day 13 Jesus, the Dividing Truth

* Hurlbert, Brandon. "The Divisiveness of Jesus." The Two Cities, August 10, 2016. https://www.thetwocities.com/practical-theology/discipleship-2/the-divisiveness-of-jesus/.

JEANINE AMAPOLA WARD is an author, speaker, podcast host, and Christian content creator from Dallas, Texas, who now lives in Oklahoma City, Oklahoma. She is the wife of Kaleb and the mother of her son, Duke. She has been in the social media industry for over a decade and has garnered more than 2.8 million followers across all platforms. She is passionate about helping women around the world know Jesus more deeply and become secure in who Christ created them to be both inside and out. Her mission is to help women live happy and healthy lives in every area—mentally, physically, spiritually, and emotionally—through God's Word and intentional daily habits. Learn more at JeanineAmapola.com.